MW01231725

The Nephilim Question: Biblical Answers

Steve McGee

WESTBOW°
PRESS
A DIVISION OF THOMAS NELSON
& ZONDERVAN

WestBow Press books may be ordered through booksellers or by contacting:

WestBow Press
A Division of Thomas Nelson & Zondervan
1663 Liberty Drive
Bloomington, IN 47403
www.westbowpress.com
1 (866) 928-1240

ISBN: 978-1-4908-3865-6 (sc)
ISBN: 978-1-4908-3866-3 (e)

Library of Congress Control Number: 2014909656

Printed in the United States of America.

WestBow Press rev. date: 10/6/2014

Table of Contents

Introduction

In the spring of 1947, a young Bedouin goat herder has lost one of his prized possessions, so he begins searching the vast cliffs along the Dead Sea. He tosses a rock into an opening of one of the caves, and instead of hearing the cries of a wayward young goat he hears the sound of clanging pottery.

The subsequent discovery that follows from the caves of Qumran is without a doubt the greatest biblical archeology discovery of our time, or any other time. 972 texts are uncovered, but it is the discovery of a little talked about scroll that I would like to draw your attention to.

The Genesis Apocryphon dates back to the second century B.C. When scholars began examining the ravaged document, what they found inside was a bit of marital disagreement, a recorded conversation between Lamech and his wife Bat- Enosh. It seems Lamech had been away on a long journey, he has returned and to his surprise and dismay and even shock, his wife Bat-Enosh has given birth to a child.

To complicate the already sticky situation, the child is extremely beautiful, and when he opens his eyes he lights up the whole house—literally!

Lamech follows the ancient traditions for marital infidelity. He condemns his wife Bat-Enosh who then in desperation explains to her husband that she has known no other man in his absence, but she also tells him this incredible statement.

"This seed came from you, and this fruit was planted by you and not by some stranger or by any of the Watchers or heavenly beings."[1]

This mention of Watchers or celestial beings is also mentioned in many other ancient texts like the book of Enoch and the sixth chapter of the book of Genesis. We will explore this in much greater detail in later chapters. The Genesis Apocryphon is one document that describes an ancient supernatural presence on the earth. It seems to be common knowledge that the Watchers, as the text states, were active in corrupting humanity at that time.

The Bible tells of a supernatural presence as well, in the tenth chapter of the book of Daniel, the Hebrew prophet is paid a visit by a celestial being, but the celestial entity is a little late arriving on the scene.

"But the prince of the kingdom of Persia withstood me twenty-one days; and behold, Michael, one of the chief princes, came to help me, for I had been left alone there with the kings of Persia." Daniel 10: 13[2]

In the context of this passage, the prince of the kingdom of Persia (which some believe is modern day Iraq), cannot be human. What held this entity up for 21 days was spiritual, and took place in a realm that is very real, but for us mostly unseen. Indeed, we are all familiar with the four dimensions of length, width, depth, and time because we deal with these dimensions every day in some kind of way. However, many scientists now tell us of as many as 10 dimensions that describe the nature and workings of the universe. Do you think we are finally starting to catch up with what was written thousands of years ago in the pages of the Bible?

"For we do not wrestle against flesh and blood, but against principalities, against powers, against the rulers of the darkness of this age, against spiritual hosts of wickedness in the heavenly places." Ephesians 6: 12³

We have heard two quick stories of the supernatural from ancient manuscripts.

Fast Forward to November 30, 2008.

Debbie (not her real name), goes to bed at approximately 2:10 in the morning. She wakes up to see a bright light coming through her bedroom window, she cannot move or speak. She is met by a tall entity and short entity. The short one is very rude, the tall one rubs her head to calm her. They communicate telepathically, they scan her body with a machine that looks like an upside down L. Usually, that is all they do, but this experience things happen to Debbie that she does not recall happening in the past ones.

She is given an injection in her upper right arm and taken to a waiting room on a stretcher. She is met next by a red-haired woman with claws on each hand. She is trustworthy and kind and Debbie is escorted to a room full of children who all run to her, from small kids to teenagers. She then is taken to another room where she sees jars of clear liquid with fetuses and embryos in them. Debbie is finally taken to a large picture window; she looks out of it and stares at war and violence being portrayed to her. Debbie then wakes up in her bed at approximately 6:00 am, and she tells her husband what she has experienced. He has not seen or experienced anything unusual.

More about the alien abduction phenomena in a later chapter, but this account is experienced almost exactly, even down to seeing people with red hair in thousands of other documented abduction cases. Sleep paralysis, bad lucid dreams, or something else?

CHAPTER 1
The Fall Before the Fall

Do you remember what you were doing in the year 1989? There is a good chance many of the readers of this book were not even born yet. Ah yes, the close of the 1980's with the big hairdo's, the popular television show "Full House", and Bruce Springsteen taught us all how to dance in the dark.

For the purpose of what I am going to talk about in this chapter, let me draw your attention to the year 1989 and to the place Tiananmen Square, the large city square in the center of Beijing, China.

For some of you out there your memory is starting to come back, for this was a major social and political event and a human interest story for the ages.

The focal point of what was going on in Tiananmen Square was that after years of oppression, horrible living conditions, and unfair economic policies, the citizens of China have made a brave and dangerous stand on the streets in and around Tiananmen Square. What is happening here is a revolt, an attempted overthrow of the totalitarian government of China by freedom loving pro democracy advocates.

The mainstream news coverage of this was intensive and many gravitated and praised the Chinese civilians that started the revolt. The end though was predictable, sad, and unfortunate. Martial law was declared by the Chinese government, the protests were controlled with military force, and large tanks began filling up the streets of Tiananmen Square. No one knows for sure, but the end result was the death of hundreds, if not thousands of Chinese civilians.

The pages of history are littered with many such revolts and uprisings against brutal and unfair governments and regimes. But now let's do something different; let us focus on something a bit strange and unusual, for indeed, biblical history begins with a revolt and an uprising. But this revolt was not against a brutal, evil, self centered government, this revolt was actually against the most perfect, complete, joyous, government in the history of all time and the history of the entire known universe.

If you turn on your television set every night and catch up on the day's news events then you know without a doubt that there truly is not much good going on in the world these days, and that makes this Scripture I am about to share sort of insightful.

The biblical character Job, many of you are familiar with his story for he underwent intense loss and suffering to himself and his possessions and his loved ones and family. In a high stakes game of cat and mouse between the Most High God and the once exalted brilliant angelic creature known as Satan, Job is questioning God's motive for all that has happened to him, he is having an open and honest conversation with God, now for God's answer.

"Where were you when I laid the foundations of the earth? Tell Me, if you have understanding. Who determined its measurements? Surely you know! Or who stretched the line upon it? To what were its foundations

fastened? Or who laid its cornerstone, When the morning stars sang together, And all the sons of God shouted for joy?" Job 38: 4-7[1]

In the context of God's answer to Job's complaints, we are told that there was a time when all of the celestial beings (sons of God) sang for joy. If we are honest with ourselves we do not know how long this heavenly state continued before Lucifer's rebellion took place. Some Bible students ponder that after the initial creation of Genesis chapter 1, verse 1, there is a gap of time before verse 2 which states the earth was void and without form, and this would account for the earth's apparent millions of years of geological ages. This is sometimes referred to as the "pre-Adamic world conditions" being that this was before Adam showed up on the biblical scene. From my perspective, we can just say that in "eternity past" there was a revolt of massive and devastating proportions which plunged the entire universe and all things seen and unseen into complete chaos. I wish there was an entire book of the Bible which deals with the fall of Satan in eternity past, but unfortunately there is not. There is no play by play account of everything that transpired. There are 2 critical Old Testament passages that give us some insight, let's look at them now.

"You were the anointed cherub who covers; I established you; You were on the holy mountain of God; You walked back and forth in the midst of fiery stones. You were perfect in your ways from the day you were created, Till iniquity was found in you." Ezekiel 28: 14-15[2]

Ezekiel chapter 28 is speaking of the very human ancient ruler of Tyre; however, there is little doubt among scholars that the above passage refers to Satan. The "fiery stones" could be the stars and planets, and the holy mountain of God could be a heavenly location.

"How you are fallen from heaven, O Lucifer, son of the morning! How you are cut down to the ground, You who weakened the

nations! For you have said in your heart: I will ascend into heaven, I will exalt my throne above the stars of God; I will also sit on the mount of the congregation On the farthest sides of the north; I will ascend above the heights of the clouds, I will be like the Most High." Isaiah 14: 12-14[3]

This created being that once walked among the fiery stones(which some see as the planets), now wants to control the very stars of God. Would you not agree that it seems Satan's most sinful attribute was self generated pride? None of us have ever struggled with that, now have we? You don't have to answer that!

In the gospel of Luke, Jesus sends out 70 followers who return extremely excited for it seems they are now able to control and cast out demons in the name of Christ, so Jesus says this:

"And He said to them, "I saw Satan fall like lightning from heaven." Luke 10: 18[4]

Now, here lies the complexity when discussing the fall of Satan. Was Jesus talking about the casting of Satan from God's presence in eternity past, which we just saw in the Ezekiel and Isaiah passages? Was Jesus describing Satan's fall in conjunction with the mission of the 70 followers that He had just sent out, or was Jesus referring to the fall of Satan in a future setting?

In the book of Job, we see the angels or heavenly host present themselves before God and Satan comes with them. So did Satan still have access to God's court in heaven even after his fall, or maybe God allowed Satan inside because He was going to let Satan begin to attack Job?

Clearly referring to the time period right before Jesus Christ's second coming, we find this passage in the book of Revelation.

"And war broke out in heaven: Michael and his angels fought with the dragon; and the dragon and his angels fought, but they did not prevail, nor was a place found for them in heaven any longer. So the great dragon was cast out, that serpent of old, called the Devil and Satan, who deceives the whole world; he was cast to the earth, and his angels were cast out with him." Revelation 12: 7-9[5]

So with all the Scriptures we have looked at, this is how we should consider the fall of Satan. In eternity past, God's most celebrated and beautiful angel, Lucifer, filled with self generated pride rebelled and attempted to overthrow the perfect universal government of God. He and his followers failed, of course, and he was cast out from the presence of God. God has let Satan back into His presence at certain times, like the attack on Job, but this author does not believe Satan has free reign into the heavenly dwelling place of God. During the time period right before the second advent of Jesus Christ, there will be war in heaven which will result in Satan being thrown to the earth, then the Scripture tells us that his time is short, and this time period will be the most horrifying and devastating in the history of the earth.

When discussing such a monumental topic like the fall of Satan, you cannot help but feel like you are oversimplifying everything, for these are monumental events which human reasoning struggles to describe.

Satan was cast from God's presence, he now is compared in Scripture to that of a roaring lion looking for whomever he can devour, and all that began in Genesis chapter 3. Satan has just deceived the man and woman, and he is given this eternal decree by God.

"And I will put enmity Between you and the woman, And between your seed and her seed; He shall bruise your head, And you shall bruise His heel." Genesis 3: 15[6]

The word enmity carries with it the condition of constant conflict, so in context of the passage there will always be conflict between the seed of the woman and the seed of the serpent. Who is the seed of the woman (Eve)? That is easy enough just read Matthew chapter 1, for it is the genealogy that saw miracle after miracle and ultimately produced the babe in the manger- Jesus Christ. But wait a second, did not the passage say that the serpent of Genesis chapter 3 has a seed also. Yes, it does!

Do you believe in intelligent evil my friend?

In 1958, Charles Starkweather along with his 14 year old girlfriend Caril Fugate went on a senseless killing spree in which 11 people were brutally murdered, some of them in the state of Nebraska. Bruce Springsteen, with just an acoustic guitar and harmonica wrote a song about the events. What makes this song entitled "Nebraska" so harrowing and chilling is that Springsteen sang the song in the first person, as if he was Charles Starkweather. In the song, the character is sitting in a prison storeroom with electric chair execution imminent. He answers the question of why he killed all those innocent people. I guess there is just a "meanness in this world."[7]

Yes, there is a "meanness in this world." The seed of the woman produced Jesus Christ, which is our only hope for an escape from the "meanness in this world". But what did the seed of the serpent produce? It produced an evil that was the very reason for the flood of the book of Genesis. This evil weaves its way into the detestable practices of the Canaanites, and later the Mayans with their unthinkable child sacrifices. This evil has continued into modern times with men like Adolf Hitler and Saddam Hussein. This evil has many names, but for the purpose of what we will reveal in the next chapters of this book, this evil can only go by one name- NEPHILIM!

CHAPTER 2

Hermeneutics and Genesis Chapter 6

Even the most conservative archaeologist will have to at some point admit there is some really weird stuff here on planet earth, left over from antiquity and our murky past history. It has been said that if you research most ancient civilizations we have writings from, you will most assuredly discover three things about that civilization. They have a story about a great flood, they have stories of dragons, and they have stories of celestial beings that descended from the skies and in many cases procreated with women. Some of these civilizations also left behind for us to ponder and scratch our heads at some pretty incredible physical left behind evidence.

It is historically and biblically accurate to state that civilization sprang up in the Middle East, around the Tigris and Euphrates rivers in a region known as the Fertile Crescent. The oldest writings we have are from a group known as the Sumerians, who appeared in this area in the third millennium B.C. The Sumerians left behind literally thousands of clay tablets and cylinders written in cuneiform script. The late Zecharia Sitchin devoted his life to interpreting Sumerian writings, and penned many bestselling books on his discoveries. I have several Sitchin books in my collection. His writings tell the stories of the Anunnaki, "Those who from Heaven to Earth came". Sitchin believes the Anunnaki from Sumerian texts are the same as the Nephilim from the Hebrew text of Genesis chapter 6, and he claims they were extraterrestrials, space travelers who came from their dying planet to earth in antiquity. Sitchin also takes the Hebrew term Adam and twists it to represent the early human species of antiquity. So in his interpretation of the Sumerian and Hebrew text, he makes the bold claim that the Anunnaki fashioned "the Adam" or the human species in their image. So to make it simple, he promotes the popular idea that mankind in the ancient past could have been created by an advanced race of extraterrestrials, in Zecharia Sitchin's case the Sumerian Anunnaki.

I have read his books and I think Zecharia Sitchin was an extremely bright scholar, and I congratulate him on his diligence and years of interpreting the Sumerian tablets. Now let me say this in as strong a way as I can, I do not share Sitchin's hermeneutic of how he interprets the Hebrew text. We are told that in the beginning God, Elohim in the Hebrew text, the standard term for deity, created the heavens and the earth. God fashioned chaos into cosmos, disorder into order, beginning and end, He sees it all and He created mankind as well. I have but one word for the theory that we were created or genetically jumpstarted by an advanced race of extraterrestrials and that word is—BLASPHEMY!

But if you are an ancient astronaut believer you still are not swayed by my rant, for there is plenty more evidence to back up your claims that mankind was visited in the ancient past. Look no further than the mysterious land of Egypt with its many pyramids, and it's most famous structure known as the Great Pyramid of Giza. One of the seven wonders of the ancient world and is believed by many to be the largest building ever erected on planet earth. The Great Pyramid of Giza weighs almost six million tons, and was constructed using 2,300,000 limestone blocks, each weighing approximately 2.5 tons. The stone blocks are so carefully fashioned that a single piece of paper will not slide between them, this is more precise than the tolerances used for the tiles on the space shuttle! Most modern architects who have studied the specifications of the Great Pyramid of Giza readily admit there is no way, even with our modern lasers and machinery that we could even come close to duplicating its construction. Yet, some Egyptologists still believe that Egyptian slaves built this incredible structure. The Great Pyramid is aligned to true north better than most modern astronomy equipment. Some are left with only one rational conclusion there is no way mankind from antiquity, with no modern technology to speak of could have built this pyramid, unless they had assistance from an advanced technologically superior race of extraterrestrials.

In Lebanon, there is a place called Baalbek located in the Bekaa Valley, this location has one of the oldest megalithic structures on earth. It has the three largest stones which are called the "Trilithon" ever to be used in a building project. These stones weigh an estimated 1000 tons each. How did early man move these stones? Baalbek has a rich history, the Greeks used the site, and then the Romans tore down the Greek's temple, and constructed their own which they dedicated to the god Jupiter. There are interestingly enough many local legends in this area of the Middle East which claim the original builders were Giants.

The ancient astronaut theory continues to this day to grow in popularity and is gaining new followers daily; the History Channel's "Ancient Aliens" series is currently in its 6th season of programs, and more are on the way. This is almost unheard of for a show on the History Channel to run that long. For Christians, the need is certainly growing to defend the reinterpretations of Scripture that are made by the ancient alien theorist.

In Exodus chapter 3, Moses encounters God in the form of a burning bush, but ancient alien theorist jump in and claim that Moses probably encountered a spaceship, and the fumes ignited the bush, so the story has been misinterpreted by the writers of Scripture.

In Ezekiel chapter 1, the prophet encounters the very throne of God descending downward in an incredible vision. If you are an ancient alien theorist then again we have a misrepresentation, for Ezekiel most certainly was witnessing an interplanetary spaceship which he could not understand.

I think I have made my point on the outright falsehoods being thrown at the Bible by the ancient alien theorist. And it only gets worse, listen to this quote from the History Channel's " Ancient Aliens" television program in an episode entitled "The Return" we have these words from researcher Steven Greer speaking on the impact of the imminent disclosure to us that extraterrestrials have been and currently are visiting mankind.

"The result would be that the fundamentalist orthodox belief systems of every organized religion on earth would collapse, meaning that it would really bring into question the origins of the human race, the Genesis stories, and a whole lot of other issues."[1]

Quite a statement, interestingly enough Zecharia Sitchin's initial interest in what would become his research began when he was a young boy in a Sunday School class, believe it or not. Sitchin had the nerve to question his teacher on the sixth chapter of the book of Genesis. The teacher hissed at young Zacharia Sitchin, told him to sit down, and not to question the Bible!

Well, as a famous college football commentator might say, "Not so fast my friend". There is another way to look at this topic and one that lines up with a face-value view of Scripture.

There are some through the years that have studied and written about the sixth chapter of Genesis from a biblical face value hermeneutic. Dr. I.D.E. Thomas wrote the standard for a Christian perspective on the UFO phenomena with his book, "The Omega Conspiracy". Chuck Missler, who has to be one of the smartest men you will ever hear speak, and yes he talks over my head too, but I love it. Chuck Missler along with Mark Eastman wrote the 1997 classic "Alien Encounters" from a Christian viewpoint.

As for the evangelical church as a whole, and I do not think I am wrong in stating this, the approach to Genesis chapter 6 can be summed up in three words: Avoidance! Avoidance! Avoidance! Well, wait a minute that is one word, no it is one word delivered three times, I think you get my point.

I became a Christian when I was 23 years old and I have attended various churches I would say pretty regularly since then. Well, I'm 50 years old now and I am still waiting to hear my first sermon from the pulpit on the sixth chapter of Genesis. I have read countless commentaries with no mention of Genesis 6; I love the writing of Bible teacher Irving L. Jensen whose books were distributed by the Moody Bible Institute. Jensen was a respected author, best known for his Bible self-study guide series, even Jensen's commentary on the book of Genesis does not even mention the main characters of the sixth chapter of Genesis. The "sons of God", the Nephilim, are not even mentioned. I have seen countless Sunday School lessons arrive at Genesis chapter 6 only to skip over the first four verses. Why avoid this pivotal section of God's precious revelation? Well, I think the reader may know why, because if you take the sixth chapter of Genesis for what it says, at face-value, then what you have is so disturbing, so unbelievable, so detestable, it is easy to choose avoidance rather than to deal with the passage. I cannot count how many times I have seen the story of Genesis chapter 3, the account of the fall of man portrayed from the pulpit, as well it should be. But my friend, the events of Genesis chapter 6 are the next major event in the biblical drama, to skip out on Genesis chapter 6 is to leave out possibly the most important pivotal moment in the entire book of Genesis and the Old Testament itself.

If there is one thing I have learned from my 50 years here on planet earth, it is that avoiding stuff whatever it is, may feel good when you are doing it, but eventually the end result will be failure, broken relationships, and regret.

As I have aged I have sort of developed a bit of a fear of high places, I had no trouble with it when I was a younger man. I went to theme parks, rode roller coasters, Ferris wheels, no problem. Imagine the butterflies in my gut when I found out at my job that I needed to start training on a Turret-Side loader, one of those massive picker forklift vehicles. I work for a pharmaceutical company so my new responsibility would be to pick up with the side loader expensive pallets of active very expensive raw materials and drugs. Thank God, I had a patient instructor for it took me about three days just to half way learn to steer the darn thing!

Every day I would come to the training sessions, I dreaded them so badly, I really wanted to avoid this training all together. To make matters worse, inside the racks where the pallets were stored was an elaborate water piping system, so as I prepared for the first time to lift off into the air about 40-50 feet upward to pick up an expensive pallet of active drug my instructor casually tells me, "One more thing, if you accidently hit one of the water lines and it leaks all over some active drug, you might as well just keep walking right out the door for you will surely be fired." No pressure, right.

I steer into the isle; luckily once I got into the correct lane I could activate a wireless remote that steered the side-loader for me. I arrive where I need to now ascend upward, I am sweating really bad, my heart is beating through my shirt, here I go. Just breathe, just breathe, you can do this.

Up I go inside the small carriage, I stop slightly above the pallet I need to pick up, and I am actually not feeling too nervous. Then I did the inevitable, I looked down! Holy crap, my heart was now beating so fast I was having difficulty catching my breath. I was now in big trouble, for my hands which had to control the delicate levers and slide the forks under the pallet were now shaking uncontrollably. I made an attempt to move the forks forward, but I had forgotten a basic training technique that was taught to me. The controls will not work unless you have your palms from each hand placed flat on the levers, which actually activates them. This was put in by the manufacturer as a safety feature that automatically keeps the drivers hands safe inside the carriage. As I tried to move the forks they would not budge, no matter what I tried, I never remembered that basic instruction. I was now a complete nervous wreck, and my instructor had to patiently guide me down. After that embarrassing disaster, I really wanted to avoid the next day's lesson but I showed up. It took me longer than any other student in the history of the program, but eventually I was certified on the side-loader and today I drive it maybe three times a week. Yes, I still get nervous, but I do it, no avoidance!

We serve a big God do we not, no need for avoidance; lets now look at the first four verses of Genesis chapter 6.

"Now it came to pass, when men began to multiply on the face of the earth, and daughters were born to them, that the sons of God saw the daughters of men, that they were beautiful; and they took wives for themselves of all whom they chose. And the Lord said, "My Spirit shall not strive with man forever, for he is indeed flesh; yet his days shall be one hundred and twenty years." There were giants on the earth in those days, and also afterward, when the sons of God came in to the daughters

of men and they bore children to them. Those were the mighty men who were of old, men of renown." Genesis 6: 1-4[2]

The obvious questions that come from these verses are: who are the "daughters of men", that is pretty easy to surmise. Who are the "sons of God" that came in to the daughters of men, and lastly who are the giants, which were the result of the union between the "sons of God" and the daughters of men? Some modern translations use the word "Nephilim" which in Hebrew means "fallen ones" to describe the offspring of the "sons of God" and daughters of men.

To answer these pressing questions we need to use the correct hermeneutic, or the right formula for translating the Bible correctly. Our principle of interpretation must be consistent without contradiction, and should lead us to ultimate truth. We need to discover the truth in this or any other key biblical text, not determine the truth by predisposed concepts of what we think the Scripture is conveying. Several years ago, I began reading the works of the late Robert Van Kampen who really championed the following concepts, but these principles were not unique to him or really anyone else for that matter. Martin Luther, during the protestant reformation proclaimed this term "sensus literalis". The Bible can be understood in its most normal and natural sense, read the Bible like you would read the morning newspaper—at face-value.

Another key principle is to understand the context of a phrase or word and it helps to know the theme of the chapter or book of the Bible in which you are studying. You need to know the historical and cultural setting where the phrase occurs also.

We need to find in the Scripture where the phrase we are studying appears again. We need to compare Scripture with Scripture to gain a full understanding and there should be no contradictions in what we have found, if there are then our interpretation is flawed, not God's inspired revelation of Scripture.

The Old Testament contains over 300 prophecies concerning the first coming of Jesus Christ; yes, some of them are duplicates and repeated often in the text. But when Jesus Christ appeared in that feed trough in Bethlehem, all of the predictions about His coming were fulfilled at face value. To discover who the "sons of God" and the "daughters of men" and the "Nephilim" are, we will use this same approach to Scripture.

Let's start with the easiest phrase from the passage to figure out, the "daughters of men". Scripture says when men began to multiply and daughters were born to them. No controversies with this, the "daughters of men" in Genesis chapter 6 are the women of the pre-flood planet earth. The passage describes them as beautiful, and I would like to take a moment here and say that as a husband to a very beautiful and lovely wife, and as the father of two fantastic daughters, not much has changed. Women are still beautiful are they not, especially Godly women, I should know because I have three of them.

The Hebrew term translated "sons of God" is "B'nai HaElohim" it is used three times in the book of Job, so let's start our search there.

"Now there was a day when the sons of God came to present themselves before the Lord, and Satan also came among them." Job 1: 6[3]

The "sons of God" here in this passage are celestial beings, the heavenly host coming to present themselves before the Holy God of the universe. This is a precursor to Satan's soon coming attacks on Job's character. So we also have him sneaking into the picture, but for the purpose of our study this is the same Hebrew phrase that we have in Genesis chapter 6 and it refers to celestial beings, angels if you please.

"Again there was a day when the sons of God came to present themselves before the Lord, and Satan came also among them to present himself before the Lord." Job 2: 1[4]

Satan will soon begin attacking Job's health, and here we have another heavenly conference. It is the same phrase that appears in Genesis chapter 6, and it refers to angels.

In fact, the New International Version English translation does not use the term "sons of God" in Job 1:6 or in Job 2:1. The New International Version uses the word "angels" as well it should, for that is what they were.

The last time the phrase "sons of God" appears in the book of Job is in chapter 38 and verse 7 and we looked at that in chapter 1. The scene is creation and all the "sons of God" shouted for joy, and once again it is the same phrase that is used in Genesis chapter 6. There is no doubt whatsoever that the passages in Job are speaking of the heavenly host or angelic beings, once again the New International Version uses the word " angels" for Job 38: 7.

Let us now look at two passages from the Psalms. David is praising God's holiness and majesty and he writes this:

"Give unto the Lord, O you mighty ones, Give unto the Lord glory and strength." Psalm 29: 1[5]

Here the phrase "O you mighty ones" means "O sons of gods," and the phrase is again speaking of spiritual beings who are in the presence of God in heaven.

"For who in the heavens can be compared to the Lord? Who among the sons of the mighty can be likened to the Lord?" Psalm 89: 6[6]

The Hebrew phrase for "the sons of the mighty" again means "sons of gods". These are heavenly beings, they are angels, and the language from these two verses in the Psalms is similar to both Job 1: 6 and Job 2: 1.

Some scholars point to the book of Daniel when a furious King Nebuchadnezzar tossed the three Israelites: Shadrach, Meshach, and Abed-Nego into the fiery furnace. The Babylonian King is astonished when he looks down and sees the three Hebrews walking in the midst of the fire, but he also sees a fourth image which the King describes in the Scripture as "like the Son of God" in Daniel 3 verse 25. I believe this was indeed a divine being. I believe the fourth image in the fire was the Lord Jesus Christ. Comparing Scripture with Scripture from the Old Testament we find strong if not conclusive evidence that the phrase "sons of God" used in the 6th chapter of Genesis is referring to celestial beings, but even stronger evidence awaits us in the New Testament.

"And the angels who did not keep their proper domain, but left their own abode, He has reserved in everlasting chains under darkness for the judgment of the great day; as Sodom and Gomorrah, and the cities around them in a similar manner to these, having given themselves over to sexual immorality and gone after strange flesh, are set forth as an example, suffering the vengeance of eternal fire." Jude 6-7[7]

The above passage from the little book of Jude is quite provocative. Who were these angels who left their own abode? Their activities are compared to Sodom and Gomorrah, these celestial beings went after strange flesh, and these particular angels are suffering the vengeance of eternal fire. By process of elimination, what other biblical event could this passage be alluding to, there seems to be no other viable alternative except the bizarre tale of the "sons of God" and daughters of men found in Genesis chapter 6.

Speaking of the certain doom of false teachers the book of 2 Peter says this:

"For if God did not spare the angels who sinned, but cast them down to hell and delivered them into chains of darkness, to be reserved for judgment; and did not spare the ancient world, but saved Noah, one of eight people, a preacher of righteousness, bringing in the flood on the world of the ungodly; and turning the cities of Sodom and Gomorrah into ashes, condemned them to destruction, making them an example to those who afterward would live ungodly;" 2 Peter 2: 4-6[8]

This passage speaks of certain angels who sinned, and even the timeframe matches the time of Noah and the flood, the ancient world where the events of Genesis chapter 6 took place. Peter's earlier epistle also puts these events in the same timeframe as Genesis chapter 6.

"by whom also He went and preached to the spirits in prison, who formerly were disobedient, when once the Divine longsuffering waited in the days of Noah, while the ark was being prepared, in which a few, that is, eight souls, were saved through water." 1 Peter 3: 19-20.[9]

These spirits in prison in which Christ proclaimed victory over were the ones who were disobedient in the days of Noah. By process of elimination, what other biblical event could the writer possibly be talking about other than the Genesis chapter 6 account?

One of the main objections to the "sons of God" being fallen angels in Genesis chapter 6 is the popular contention that angels are spirit beings, which therefore are incapable of marrying or coming even close to the events described in Genesis chapter 6. Many will point to the gospel of Matthew chapter 22 when Jesus states that at the resurrection there will be no marriage in the same way as we have today. Jesus goes on to say people will be like the angels in heaven.

That viewpoint is easily cast aside when you realize that Christ was speaking of the angels in heaven and the angels from the Genesis 6 passage had forfeited their place in heaven, they had rebelled with Lucifer, indeed, they were the angels who sinned.

Traditionally speaking, angels are portrayed as ministering mostly invisible spirit beings and this may sound good on a Hallmark card, but it falls incredibly short on biblical truth.

The two angels who arrived in Sodom to warn Lot of the soon coming destruction did not wear bright halos of amber white and they did not have wings, the Bible tells us that they looked like men. In many angelic appearances in both the Old Testament and the New Testament angels took the form of men. Lot baked the two angels he entertained bread and the angels ate it in Genesis 19 and verse 3. In the story of Sodom and Gomorrah the wicked men wanted to have sex with the angels, so indeed, they looked like men. The angels that left their first estate that being heaven, and came into the daughters of men in the ancient past, in my opinion, did not look like big headed thin alien type creatures with the big almond eyes as in "Close Encounters of the Third Kind" fame. It is logical and the biblical evidence points to these angels taken on very human form.

"Do not forget to entertain strangers, for by so doing some have unwittingly entertained angels." Hebrews 13: 2[10]

My wife tells a great story that took place years ago when she lived in Greensboro, North Carolina. The church she attended had a very vibrant college and career ministry, and on Sunday nights they would meet at a little house that was fairly close to the church.

They just gathered at this house and prayed for one another, word of mouth spread and soon many people from other churches and fellowships began coming to these prayer meetings.

One particular Sunday night, the large group was deep in prayer when suddenly the front door opened and in walked an African-American gentleman who instructed the group that God told him to come to this house for some refreshment and prayer. He prayed with the group and left, now keep in mind that this house had no advertisements announcing the prayer meeting and no one invited this man, and no one from the group even knew this man, or had ever seen him before. It goes without saying that the unlikely visitor was never seen again to my wife's knowledge by anyone from the prayer group. Was this man an angel? We will never know the answer to that, but angels are quite extraordinary entities. In the Old Testament, one single angel was responsible for the deaths of 185,000 Syrians. They are capable of great power!

It has been pointed out by some that the term "sons of God" appears in the New Testament, and always refers to believers, that is true but keep this simple fact in perspective, it is not the same word connotation, or even the same language for that matter, for the Old Testament was written in Hebrew and the New Testament in Greek. In order to be called a son of God in the New Testament you must be a born again believer (Romans 8:14), and when you invite Jesus Christ into your heart and life, a divine miracle takes place and you become a new creation. The Scriptures declare you are a child of God, but it is not the same usage and meaning as the Hebrew "B'nai HaElohim" which describes the angelic "sons of God".

Concerning the offspring of the "sons of God" and daughters of men we find most English translations like the popular New King James version(which I am quoting from in this book), translate the offspring as "giants". But this word is from the Hebrew "Nephilim" and literally means "the fallen ones" from the Hebrew verb "nephal" meaning "to fall." In the Septuagint translation, the term was applied as "gigantes" or "earth-born" and that is a big reason our modern

English translations translate the word giants for the Hebrew word Nephilim. They are also called "Hag Gibborim" meaning "the mighty ones".

Genesis 6:4 has the very ominous phrase "there were giants on the earth in those days, and also afterwards", so one could easily assume that the bizarre events involving celestial beings procreating with human women occurred again. This is the topic of much heated debate among Christian scholars looking into the question of the Nephilim and possible other incursions found in the Scriptures.

In the book of Numbers chapter 13, Moses sends out spies into the land of Canaan and in verse 33 they report back seeing the giants in the land. The spies claimed these post-flood Nephilim were so tall that they looked like grasshoppers in their sight; in chapter 4 we will take a long look at this passage.

So taking Scripture in context, and comparing Scripture with Scripture, it is this author's conclusion that the "daughters of men" were the women from antiquity who inhabited the earth. The "sons of God" were celestial beings or fallen angels who left their first estate, which was heaven, and procreated with the "daughters of men". The results of this unholy union were the "Nephilim" who were monstrous tyrants of great size and strength.

I will also point out with great confidence that the early church fathers would have agreed with me.

"They made God their enemy; for many angels of God accompanied with women, and begat sons that proved unjust, and despisers of all that was good, on account of the confidence they had in their own strength, for the tradition is that these men did what resembled the acts of those whom the Grecians call giants."[11] Jewish historian Josephus.

Justin Martyr, Irenaeus, and Tertullian would have agreed with me also. It is a historically accurate statement to say the early church fathers and the ancient Hebrew scholars understood the text to refer to celestial beings procreating with human women. The "face-value" approach began to change in the fifth century A.D. The theology of Romanism was beginning to triumph, and the worship of angels had begun within the church, and celibacy was now a popular institution in the Roman Catholic Church. The "angel" view of Genesis chapter 6, although being the correct way to interpret the text from a literal, face-value position was now being thrown aside for a better fit to the doctrines of Romanism. Augustine was one of the first to teach this alternative interpretation, and this interpretation of Genesis chapter 6 survived into the middle ages and it is still taught today in our modern seminaries and Christian schools, we know it as "The Sethite view".

In Genesis chapter 4, we are told the history of Adam's first two sons. When we come to Genesis chapter 5, we are introduced to Adam's third son whose name was Seth. The Sethite view teaches that the account in Genesis chapter 6 refers to a failure to keep the "faithful" lines of Seth away from the "wordly" or ungodly lines of Cain. The theory's logic is that after Cain killed Abel, the Sethites remained faithful while the line of Cain became evil, rejected God, and became horribly rebellious. So the "sons of God" are faithful men from Seth's lineage and the "daughters of men" are wicked women from the line of Cain. Why the children from these unions turned out to be giant, monstrous creatures known as the Nephilim goes without explanation in the Sethite view.

As we have learned, the Hebrew phrase for the "sons of God" is translated "B'nai HaElohim", "sons of Elohim," and it is a phrase used consistently in the Old Testament for angels. The early church fathers taught this and the ancient rabbinical sources understood the term to be speaking of the angels. If the text was demonstrating the mixed marriages of the line of Seth and the line of Cain then why does the text simply state that? The text should logically say "sons of Seth" and "daughters of Cain" if the Sethite view is to have any validity. The Sethite view is obviously guilty of inserting into the text something that a literal, face-value interpretation does not allow for.

Also, there is no Scriptural evidence that the line of Seth was all that moral or godly. In the book of Genesis, only the patriarch Enoch and Noah's immediate family of eight people were saved and there is no evidence that the wives of Noah's sons were from the line of Seth.

A face-value approach to the phrase "daughters of men" clearly shows that these women were from all corners of the known world of antiquity, not just from the lineage of Cain as the Sethite view teaches. The text would have proclaimed "the daughters of Cain" if that were true.

Perhaps the most fatal flaw of the Sethite view is the unnatural offspring that were produced.It is true that believers marrying unbelievers can result in some rebellious, mischievous children, but I do not think the result would be giant, monstrous, hybrid creatures known as the Nephilim.

The Sethite view was and is popular for one main reason and that is because understanding chapter 6 of the book of Genesis at face-value is hard to believe. It shows the reader just what Satan and his followers are capable of and it highlights the way we like to look at the spiritual world. We want to keep it invisible and say that intelligent evil never openly manifests and appears plainly in front of us. My dear friend, if you keep reading the contents of this book, you are going to discover, without a doubt, that line of thinking is absolutely false!

The Genesis invasion of evil fallen angels was part of a bigger plan of the evil one in his cosmic battle with the Lord Jesus Christ. Many

Bible scholars place the arrival of the fallen angels at the time of Jared, and if this is true then what we are looking at is possibly 300 plus years of direct contact with the human race. That is really hard to conceive or think about, and it was difficult for the creator God to deal with this as well. But God had the ultimate answer to stop this unnatural incursion that was going to contaminate the entire human race, and that answer was—the Flood!

In Genesis chapter 6 and verse 9 we read this concerning Noah.

"This is the genealogy of Noah. Noah was a just man, perfect in his generations. Noah walked with God." Genesis 6: 9[12]

When it comes to biblical interpretation, I believe that the Scriptures as they appeared in their original manuscripts were absolutely the infallible word of God, and they are without major content error. The above verse is a great example of how our modern English translations sometimes miss the mark of the intended meaning of the passage. To state it another way, sometimes our English translations of certain passages just do not go far enough with the passage. The Hebrew word for "perfect" in Genesis 6:9 means "without blemish, unimpaired". The word is used for physical blemishes or defects in the Old Testament. How enlightening to our study, for it would seem that Noah was "perfect in his generations" so Noah's immediate family was not contaminated by the activities of the "sons of God."

The fantastic Bible teacher, Chuck Missler, often says that if the only reason for the worldwide flood of Noah's day was that people were evil or wicked, then we all better get lifejackets!

This was a satanic attack on humanity for if the bloodlines of the human race were contaminated, then Satan and his emissaries could overrun planet earth. More importantly, the promised seed of the woman from Genesis chapter 3 would never have been born, that being God in the flesh, Jesus Christ. We often read the first chapter of the gospel of Matthew, and we read the long list of genealogies and we may think to ourselves "this is so boring". In fact, what the long listing of the line of people that would lead to the birth of the Messiah is really telling us is that Satan's many attempts to stop Jesus Christ from ever coming to earth in human form, that is fully God and fully man did not work, and that my friend is not boring at all!

After the flood, we have the beginning of the kingdom of Babel and in Genesis 10:8 we read this concerning Nimrod.

"Cush begot Nimrod; he began to be a mighty one on the earth." Genesis 10: 8[13]

The Hebrew word for "mighty one" in the above passage is "gibborim" which is similar to the language of Genesis chapter 6 which describes the Nephilim. So was Nimrod a supernaturally inspired demonic tyrant?

What Nimrod would go on to achieve in defiance of God is the building of the tower of Babel which was a vain attempt to "reach unto heaven" (Genesis 11:4). It is widely known that astrology and the zodiac trace their beginnings to the activities of Nimrod and the tower of Babel. It is with Nimrod that the false "mother and son" worship system started. Ancient writings reveal that Nimrod's wife Semiramis claimed to have been impregnated by a sunbeam and Semiramis gave birth to a son named Tammuz. This was an early attempt at a counterfeit virgin birth. One day while out hunting, Tammuz was tragically killed by a wild boar. Semiramis was grief stricken and the legend says that she cried and would not eat for 40 days, after this time her son Tammuz legend says was miraculously raised from the dead. This was the beginning of the systematic "mystery" religion of Babylon. Similar accounts to the story of Nimrod and Semiramis and Tammuz would populate the ancient world's false religious systems and mythologies. In Assyria, we have the Queen Ishtar and her son was Bacchus. In Egypt, we have the Queen Isis and her son was Osiris. In ancient Greece, we have the tale of Aphrodite and her son Eros; and in Roman mythology we have the Queen Venus and her son Cupid.

The belief in Mary as the virgin and co-mediator with Christ as proclaimed by the Roman Catholic Church is another example of this false religious system which was started by Nimrod at the tower of Babel. Please note I am critical of the system, not the majority of the people. I know there are many outstanding Catholic believers in our world today.

In the book of Revelation chapter 17, John identifies Rome as "MYSTERY, BABYLON" and this false religious system which is responsible for the deaths of countless people throughout the centuries will finally be destroyed by God.

So if Nimrod was a supernaturally enhanced "Nephilim" does that mean that the Antichrist will also be a "Nephilim" when he appears at the end of the age? We will explore that question in a later chapter.

The contents of this chapter are indeed controversial and fascinating. Let me throw in this precaution, one's view on the identity of the "sons of God" and the "Nephilim" is not a salvation issue. If there is truly extraterrestrial life in the universe it will not invalidate Christianity. You can adhere to the Sethite view and still be in good standing with God.

Concerning the sixth chapter of Genesis, Christian researcher Tom Horn states the following in his book, "Nephilim Stargates":

"Regardless of one's interpretation of this particular verse, thousands of years ago heavenly beings visited the earth. They engaged in experiments resulting in a race of mutant offspring called Nephilim. In the New Testament, Jesus Christ speaks of these days (of Noah) as being comparable to the time leading up to his return and to the end of the age (Matt. 24:37). Are current "UFO" visitors, and resultant abductions and experiments, the same as those of Noah's day? If so, why have heavenly beings visited (and continue visiting) the earth, and what is this genetic tinkering with creation about?"[14]

Is there evidence outside of the Bible that speaks of the Nephilim, we will cover that in the next chapter.

CHAPTER 3

Nephilim History

Identifying the "sons of God" from the sixth chapter of Genesis as fallen angels or celestial beings has certainly been demonstrated by many capable Bible scholars in the past. In fact, it would appear that a face-value reading of the text when compared with others in the Scriptures leaves one with the inescapable conclusion that at some time in the history, or really the correct term is pre-history of planet earth beings descended from the heavens and procreated with human females.

There is a view of Genesis chapter 6 from Orthodox Judaism that asserts the "sons of God" were very human "nobles" or "magnates". This speculation follows the traditions that come from the ancient near east, but like "the Sethite view" that comes from Christian history, this view obviously inserts into the text what is not there.

Now, I would like the reader to indulge me for a little exercise into my take on ancient mythology. Picture yourself standing in your front yard; now fast forward your line of thinking 2000 years into the future. Now, I think we can say with absolute certainty that

2000 years from right now you will not be around to stand in your front yard, and your front yard will not look the same in 2000 years as it does now.

Now, let us say that in 2000 years from right now in the area of ground that used to be your front yard someone is walking around with a shovel in his hand, and he digs this up out of the ground.

A headline from a tabloid publication stating that Elvis Presley was seen pumping gas into his car at the corner gas station in Clayton, North Carolina on this date September 8, 2013.

Modern tabloid weekly magazines are notorious for printing and publishing sensationalized stories about famous movie stars. So, if the above story was uncovered 2000 years from now a fact check would discover that a real person named Elvis Presley did actually exist. His lifespan was from January 8, 1935 to August 16, 1977. Elvis Presley was a very famous singer and performer. His moniker was "the King of Rock and Roll" and he was one of the first performers to take the fusion of rhythm and blues and convert it into what would become modern rock and roll music, and what he could do with his hips still makes many women faint.

So this imaginary document that was dug up in what used to be your front yard 2000 years from now is not factually correct. If Elvis Presley died on August 16, 1977, then he could not have been seen pumping gas in Clayton, North Carolina on September 8, 2013. Elvis Presley was and is so popular that many false stories have been generated about him, and some of those myths include stories that Elvis Presley did not actually die. But he was a real person, who lived a real life, so inside that imaginary document that was unearthed 2000 years into the future, we would find a false story that was based on a very real truth. My friend, that is what we find in all the myths and stories we have from our mythologies.

Clay tablets from the Sumerians describe the interbreeding of their gods with human women.

The Incas believe they came from the "sons of the Sun".

The South Sea Islanders trace their ancestry to gods who visited them in a gigantic glowing egg.

In India, we have the famous Sanskrit texts which tell of gods fathering children with the women of earth.

In mythologies we find from almost every ancient culture and people group on planet earth, there is an "original revelation" to which these myths come from and it is the story from the Bible that tells of celestial beings the "sons of God" who came into the daughters of men, and they had children who were abnormal creatures of antiquity known as the Nephilim.

Many of us are quite familiar with Greek mythology and interestingly enough the legend of the Genesis 6 events roll through the Greek myths. In Greek mythology, we have numerous tales of the gods having sexual relations with mere mortals and producing half-god, half-man demigods. The most famous of the gods in Greek mythology is Zeus and his seductions included Thetis, Leda, and Metis. Wow, Zeus was quite a player! The Genesis chapter 6 narrative describes the exploits of the Nephilim as "mighty men who were of old, men of renown". By far, the best non biblical literature that speaks of the Nephilim is found in the apocryphal book of Enoch. Hang on to your bootstraps, this stuff is fascinating, but a word of caution before we dive in.

"All Scripture is given by inspiration of God, and is profitable for doctrine, for reproof, for correction, for instruction in righteousness, that the man of God may be complete, thoroughly equipped for every good work." 2 Timothy 3: 16-17[1]

For everything we can glean from the book of Enoch, we must remember that it is not canon. The book is not inspired Scripture. However, we must also conclude that the book was very important to the early church. The New Testament book of Jude quotes from the book of Enoch concerning the coming of Messiah to execute judgment on the ungodly. Jude had access to the book of Enoch, and he did not hesitate to quote from it, and God inspired him to do that.

Many scholars say that the book could not have been written by the Enoch of the Bible, but was written at a much later date probably around the second century. The author added the name Enoch for good publicity purposes. Enoch is only mentioned four times in the Bible, he is the seventh of the ten patriarchs between Adam and Noah. He is also the father of Methuselah who lived to be 969 years of age. Enoch was known as a very godly individual and strangely enough the Bible says Enoch did not die a natural death. It is recorded that Enoch walked with God and then God took him to heaven. Enoch experienced an individualized rapture of being translated to heaven without his heart stopping first.

The book of Enoch refers to the angels by the term "watchers" and this word is used in the book of Daniel.

"I saw in the visions of my head while on my bed, and there was a watcher, a holy one, coming down from heaven." Daniel 4: 13[2]

This was King Nebuchadnezzar's second vision recorded in the book of Daniel. The book of Enoch actually records where the fallen angels of the sixth chapter of Genesis landed when they first descended to planet earth.

"And it came to pass when the children of men multiplied that in those days were born unto them beautiful and comely daughters. And the angels, the children of the heaven, saw and lusted after them, and said to one another: "Come, let us choose us wives from among the children of men and beget us children". And Semjaza, who was their leader, said unto them: "I fear ye will not indeed agree to do this deed, and I alone shall have to pay the penalty of a great sin." And they all answered and said. "Let us all swear an oath and all bind ourselves by mutual imprecations not to abandon this plan but to do this thing." Then sware they all together and bound themselves by mutual imprecations. And they were in all two hundred who descended in the days of Jared on the summit of Mount Hermon."[3]

The above passage from the book of Enoch certainly adds specifics to the Genesis account in the Bible. The angels lusted for the women of earth just like the Genesis 6 passage says also. The leader of the fallen angels "Semjaza", is named as well as the number of fallen angels who descended which was 200. I think personally that it was 200 fallen angels in this initial incursion, but more had to follow in later months. The location of this initial invasion is also named and it was the summit of Mount Hermon. Mount Hermon is located near the ancient city of Damascus in what is today modern Syria. In the gospel of Matthew, Jesus Christ made the proclamation that the "gates of hell" will not stop His Church. Jesus made this famous statement in a place called Caesarea Philippi, which is located at the base of the southwest slope of Mount Hermon. Wow! This place has a vast history of idol worship and paganism, could Jesus have picked this place to declare his Messianic revelations as a signal to the forces of evil that things were about to change?

The book of Enoch states that the fallen angels first appeared in the days of Jared. We know from the book of Genesis that Jared was part of Noah's lineage and he lived to be 962 years of age. From Jared until the time of Noah and the subsequent flood we can estimate approximately 300 plus years of fallen angels in direct contact with human beings on planet earth.

The book of Enoch goes on to claim that the fallen angels instructed the people of earth in the use of charms and the arts of magic. The book of Enoch records that the fallen angels instructed the women of earth in the use of cosmetics, the next time you are late for an event and your wife is still in the bathroom, think about that!

The book of Enoch also says that one of the fallen angels showed women how to kill the embryo in the womb. That should send chills up every person's spine that loves the Lord Jesus Christ! Not much has changed, has it?

In Chapter 15 of the book of Enoch we read this:

"Now the giants, who have been born of spirit and of flesh, shall be called upon earth evil spirits, and on earth shall be their habitation. Evil spirits shall proceed from their flesh, because they were created from above; from the holy Watchers was their beginning and primary foundation. Evil spirits shall they be upon earth, and the spirits of the wicked shall they be called. The habitation of the spirits of heaven shall be in heaven; but upon earth shall be the habitation of terrestrial spirits, who are born on earth. The spirits of the giants shall be like clouds, which shall oppress, corrupt, fall, contend, and bruise those upon earth."[4]

It has always been popular in Christian tradition to accept that fallen angels and demons are the same type of creatures, but that is not what many in the early church thought. The above passage from the book of Enoch claims that the spirits of the giants or Nephilim will remain on the earth as demonic spirits.

Did this happen when the Nephilim were destroyed in the Flood of Noah? Did the spirits of the Nephilim become the demons we read about in the New Testament and our still with us today?

Remember when Jesus in the gospel of Matthew casts out demons, which quickly went into a herd of swine. It would appear that demons are disembodied spirits who wreck havoc in our physical realm. It would also appear that fallen angels are different than demons, for they can manifest in any form they choose to, and more often than not angels are mistaken for men when they manifest in the pages of the Bible.

Finally, the book of Enoch records that in the days before their ultimate destruction in the Flood of Noah; the Nephilim actually turned to cannibalism and began to devour each other's flesh. This would add light to the Genesis chapter 6 account which states that God could no longer accept the wickedness of man on the earth in those days.

Other ancient sources mention the Nephilim like the book of Jubilees and the Zadokite Document. So the Nephilim were all destroyed in the flood, so how does one explain the giants that were in the land of Canaan? We cover that topic in our next chapter.

CHAPTER 4

Giants in the Land of Canaan

My apologies to Las Vegas, Nevada but the original "sin city" had to be in my mind the biblical land of Canaan. If you could take a stroll through these ancient lands you could look to your right and see open prostitution being displayed, and you could look to your left and see a group of worshipers conjuring up evil spirits with the art of witchcraft.

Just like the time before the Noahic Flood, God predicted that the awful practices of the Canaanites would one day reach their full measure and retribution from a Holy God would ensue.

"But in the fourth generation they shall return here, for the iniquity of the Amorites is not yet complete." Genesis 15: 16[1]

When that rag tag, dirty, smelly, scrawny, group of Israelites began to surround the land of Canaan the promised retribution for the sins of the Amorites was about ready to start. Just how bad and evil were the wicked people groups that made up the land of Canaan? Let us now listen to the words of Moses recorded in the book of Deuteronomy.

"There shall not be found among you anyone who makes his son or his daughter pass through the fire, or one who practices witchcraft, or a soothsayer, or one who interprets omens, or a sorcerer, or one who conjures spells, or a medium, or a spiritist, or one who calls up the dead. For all who do these things are an abomination to the Lord, and because of these abominations the Lord your God drives them out from before you." Deuteronomy 18: 10-12[2]

The above passage mentions not to let your son or daughter "pass" through the fire. One of the false gods in the land was a god named Moloch, his image was such that he sat with his arms extended and a fire burning on his lap, babies and toddlers were sacrificed to Moloch and this is mentioned in the Old Testament. As you can see from reading the above passage almost every occult activity was alive and vibrant in the land of Canaan. Moses warning not to get enticed by all that was, of course, neglected by many of the Israelites, and their disobedience became the backdrop for so much Old Testament Scripture.

Canaan was the bridge that connected the ancient world and the region linked the lands of Egypt and Mesopotamia. The Canaanites were a mixed group of peoples and religions. The Canaanites worshiped many gods; their chief god was El who was the father of all gods and mortals. Baal was the storm god and was the most powerful of the Canaanite gods. Ashtoreth was the female fertility goddess and she is closely associated with the storm god Baal and she was also linked with the stars.

There should be no doubt that the land of Canaan was a virtual cesspool of evil. Who was running the show in the land of Canaan? Moses tells us very plainly.

"They sacrificed to demons, not to God, To gods they did not know, To new gods, new arrivals That your fathers did not fear." Deuteronomy 32: 17[3]

So when the Israelites are almost set to begin to enter this land of Canaan they are going up against the very soldiers of hell itself, demonic hordes of every detestable act and practice imaginable. God has promised them that He would pay back the sin of the Amorites, and just who are the Amorites, well my friend, the Amorites were GIANTS!

Within Christendom there are basically three controversies or points of disagreement when it comes to the subject of the Nephilim and the "sons of God". We looked in chapter 2 at the first debate that comes up and that is just who are the "sons of God" and the Nephilim from the Genesis chapter 6 passage. By taking the verses in context and comparing Scripture with other Scripture I have concluded that the "sons of God" from Genesis are fallen angels, and that the Nephilim were giants. The other popular interpretation says the "sons of God" were faithful Sethites and that the daughters of men from the Genesis 6 passage were evil women from the line of Cain. The fallen angels who procreated with the daughters of men it is said in the New Testament book of Jude are now in everlasting chains awaiting their ultimate judgment from God. So we can conclude that these specific angels from Genesis 6 are no longer free to do their nasty deeds on planet earth. We also know that the flood was God's form of judgment for the evil of men's hearts and that except for eight people, everyone and every living creature at that time was utterly destroyed and that would have included the pre-flood Nephilim. Another controversy surrounds end time prophecy and a possible "Return of the Nephilim" and we will discuss that in a later chapter.No one doubts that there were people in the land of Canaan that were extremely tall and strong, for there are many Bible passages that say that very thing. The point of contention comes from the question of just how the giants arrived in the land of Canaan, was it by natural means, or was it by supernatural means just like the events of Genesis chapter 6? That is the second controversy concerning the Nephilim among Christians. To unpack this, let's now look at the

Bible Scripture we have recorded on the giants that inhabited the land of Canaan.

It is now 400 plus years after the flood and we read this in the book of Genesis.

"In the fourteenth year Chedorlaomer and the kings that were with him came and attacked the Rephaim in Ashteroth Karnaim, the Zuzim in Ham, the Enim in Shaveh Kiriathaim," Genesis 14: 5[4]

This raid against the Rephaim is an early indication that people of large stature were already in the land of Canaan. In Hebrew, the word Rephaim comes from the term Rapha which means "fearful one; giant".

More giant tribes are mentioned in the first two chapters of the book of Deuteronomy.

"{The Emim had dwelt there in times past, a people as great and numerous and tall as the Anakim. They were also regarded as giants, like the Anakim, but the Moabites call them Emim." Deuteronomy 2: 10-11[5]

The Emim in Hebrew means "terrible ones", and the Anakim which the passage calls giants were descendents of Anak which translates as "long-necked; giant".

Now, let's look at the most important passage in the Bible concerning giants in the Promised Land. In the book of Numbers chapter 13, God instructs Moses to send spies into the land of Canaan, from what we have learned about the land of Canaan, I do not think the Israelites were forming lines for this assignment. Moses sends out 12 spies in this dramatic moment of biblical history. Moses tells them to bring back a report on the land, are the people there strong or weak. Are there many or few, what do their cities look like, and with it being the time for the grape harvest Moses tells them to bring a cluster back from the land.

"Then they came to the Valley of Eshcol, and there cut down a branch with one cluster of grapes; they carried it between two of them on a pole. They also brought some of the pomegranates and figs." Numbers 13: 23[6]

So it took two Israelites to carry this cluster of grapes on a pole between them. This was no doubt an enormous cluster of grapes. Big people need big food and we have to ask this question, was this a early example of genetic modification by the wicked giants who inhabited the land of Canaan?

After forty days of spying, they returned to Moses and Aaron and all the congregation of Israel with the findings of their sojourn. The people there are strong and the cities are fortified and very large, then the spies told the Israelite congregation that was listening intently and hanging on their every descriptive word a very incredible statement.

"And they gave the children of Israel a bad report of the land which they had spied out, saying, "The land through which we have gone as spies is a land that devours its inhabitants, and all the people whom we saw in it are men of great stature. There we saw the giants (the descendants of Anak came from the giants); and we were like grasshoppers in our sight, and so we were in their sight." Numbers 13: 32-33[7]

The word giants in the above Scripture is translated as Nephilim in other translations like the New International Version. So in essence, 10 of the 12 spies reported that they saw in the land of Canaan the descendants of the Nephilim, and there was no way they were going to engage these creatures in any type of warfare.

So here we have in these two verses the very heart of the debate concerning giants in the land of Canaan.

"(That was also regarded as a land of giants; giants formerly dwelt there. But the Ammonites call them Zamzummim," Deuteronomy 2: 20[8]

People of large stature were in the land, there is no denying that biblical fact, but how did they get there? Some say the giant tribes from the land of Canaan were ordinary human beings who suffered from the medical condition known as gigantism. This condition is characterized by above average growth and height and what causes gigantism is the over production of a growth hormone. Gigantism is hereditary and could have affected entire tribes in the land of Canaan.

Some say the giants in the land of Canaan were the result of another incursion of celestial beings in similar fashion to the time before the flood. The Genesis 6 fallen angels have been put in everlasting confinement and the Nephilim from the pre- Flood world were all destroyed, so this proposed invasion would not be the same angels or Nephilim that we had in Genesis chapter 6. There is no specific Scripture that says the giants in Canaan were ordinary humans who suffered from gigantism, and on the other hand, there is no specific Scripture that details another invasion of fallen angels in the land of Canaan. So that is why we have this debate, let us now dig deeper into the account of the spies as recorded in Numbers chapter 13 and 14.

Numbers chapter 13 and verse 4 tells us that the spies gave the children of Israel a "bad report", and that was that the land was filled with terrible and gigantic Nephilim giants. In chapter 14, we read that the people wept that very night and even wished to return back to Egypt and back to slavery. Moses and Aaron fell on their faces in front of the whole assembly of Israelites who refused to trust God. Then it is recorded that the two faithful spies Joshua and Caleb spoke out and proclaimed that the land was indeed a good land, a land that flows with milk and honey. They also said do not fear the people in the land for we have the protection of the Lord. Moses interceded on behalf of unfaithful Israel, but they were relegated to move about aimlessly in the wilderness for 40 years. The punishment corresponded to the spies 40 day trip into the land of Canaan.

"Now the men whom Moses sent to spy out the land, who returned and made all the congregation complain against him by bringing a bad report of the land, those very men who brought the evil report about the land, died by the plague before the Lord. But Joshua the son of Nun and Caleb the son of Jephunneh remained alive, of the men who went to spy out the land." Numbers 14: 36-38[9]

So of the 12 spies only two were spared Joshua and Caleb. So does that mean the "bad report" was a lie? Please notice that Joshua and Caleb never during the entire drama accused the other 10 of lying. I think the more logical way to explain this is that the 10 spies that were ultimately given a death sentence were killed for their unbelief in what God had already promised these people He would do for them, and that was help them defeat the people of the land. It is hard to believe that the giants they encountered were so tall that they made them look like mere insects in their presence. The spies feared the giants that were in the land of Canaan, so if they exaggerated the giant's actual height and strength it would get the rest of the Israelites to join their cause for not going into the land. Exaggerations of already incredible encounters actually are quite common, and have also been found to be true in regards to the ongoing UFO phenomena.

Eventually, the Israelites did go into the land of Canaan under the leadership of Joshua and began to destroy the giant tribes in the land. We read in the Bible that one giant remained of the remnant and that was Og king of Bashan, and in this Scripture we get our best clue as to just how tall these giants in Canaan really were.

"For only Og king of Bashan remained of the remnant of the giants. Indeed his bedstead was an iron bedstead. (Is it not in Rabbah of the

people of Ammon?) Nine cubits is its length and four cubits its width, according to the standard cubit." Deuteronomy 3: 11[10]

So it is interesting that we are not told how tall Og king of Bashan was in this passage, but his bedstead was nine cubits in its length and four cubits in its width. Nine cubits according to the New King James version study Bible would have been approximately 13 feet, also four cubits would have been six feet based on the standard cubit which was about 18 inches. So the bedstead was 13 feet long and six feet wide! So we can assume Og king of Bashan was a little shorter than his bedstead unless he enjoyed sleeping with his legs and feet hanging over the bedstead. If Og king of Bashan were around today he maybe would go in the first round of the NBA draft, but then again, he would probably attempt to eat the opposing teams players.........
Literally! The Scriptures declare that Og's kingdom extended from the river Arnon to Mount Hermon. Remember that Mount Hermon was the place where the fallen angels first landed when they arrived on planet earth according to the book of Enoch. Og King of Bashan was no doubt an evil giant tyrant, in fact, when Joshua's armies began destroying Og's kingdom they left no one in it alive.

"And we utterly destroyed them, as we did to Sihon king of Heshbon, utterly destroying the men, women, and children of every city." Deuteronomy 3: 6[11]

Here we have one of the greatest areas of criticism from teachers and secular scholars who aim to discredit the Bible. Why would a God who champions love and grace and forgiveness instruct Joshua on several occasions in the Old Testament to completely kill all the people of the tribe, not only the men but even women, and innocent children as well? We know ancient cultures practiced what was called blood retribution so even if one family member remained alive that person was bound by this tribal law to always seek revenge against the people who killed his family and others in the specific tribe. So some say God was showing mercy to completely wipe out the tribe and thus end the pattern of violence that would continue endlessly. That explanation does not go far enough in explaining why God ordered Joshua to kill off all men, women, and children; indeed, I ask would a small innocent child be filled with revenge? As we have mentioned earlier there are some scholars both secular and Christian that would explain that the giants in the land of Canaan suffered from the medical condition known as gigantism, which is hereditary, so it was so bad that entire tribes of men, women, and children would have been afflicted with this painful genetic disorder, so out of mercy God ordered their destruction. That still does not explain why God ordered the complete destruction of all the people. Today there are plenty of people who have genetic disorders and live with pain every day of their lives, and they would find no mercy in having their lives snuffed out before them out of alleged kindness from God. Finally, some would say that God ordered all the people in certain tribes to be killed because they were just so evil. Yes, they were evil no questioning that fact, but wait just a second here, were not the people of Nineveh described as exceedingly wicked and yet God still sent a reluctant Jonah to preach to these wicked people and lead them in the direction of morality and Godliness. The fact that the people in Canaan were wicked would not answer the question of why God ordered Joshua to completely and without any form of mercy destroy them all.

I remember teaching a Sunday School class years ago and I had in my class a very nice husband and wife. One Sunday morning they met me in the church hallway as I was about to enter the room, and they warned me that their daughter who was a sophomore in college was visiting them that weekend. She was with them at church and she would be attending my class that morning, and they cautioned me to be ready for their daughter was not a Christian and was very antagonistic in regards to the tenants of Christianity. It did not take her long as I started into my lesson to proclaim that the God of the Old Testament and the God of the New Testament were indeed two separate entities. The God described in the Old Testament was very cruel and heartless for He instructed the Israelites to kill women and children, but on the other hand, the God of the New Testament was always portrayed as loving, patient, and so very kind to all who follow Him.

It is a difficult question to attempt to answer, but let me take you back to Genesis chapter 3 and the eternal decree that was given to the woman and the serpent, that there would always be constant conflict between the seed of the woman and the seed of the serpent. The promised seed of the woman would over time result in the earthly appearance of the Messiah, Jesus Christ. The seed of the serpent would consume most of the Old Testament narrative trying to destroy the people of the seed of the woman. I believe, as do others, that Satan established the giants in the Promised Land of Canaan in a strategic fashion hoping they would ultimately destroy all of the Israelites, and in so doing, stop the very bloodline that would produce Jesus Christ.

This will never be a popular theory in the Christian world, but if there was a second incursion of fallen angelic beings in the land of Canaan, then the same action would need to be taken by a Holy God as was taken in the days before the flood. That would be a complete destruction of the affected people. The problem would then become a "gene contamination problem," and to let it continue would result in the extermination of the human race.

Under the skillful leadership of Joshua, the giants were defeated with Og king of Bashan and his vast kingdom being the ultimate prize. So we can glean from the Scriptures that the land in the mountains of Judah was giant-free thanks to the Israelites. However, this does not end the saga of giants in the Old Testament.

"None of the Anakim were left in the land of the children of Israel; they remained only in Gaza, in Gath, and in Ashdod." Joshua 11: 22[12]

As we have mentioned already the Anakim were descendents from Anak, which in Hebrew translates as "long-necked; giant". So the Bible states that some giants at that time remained outside of the land of Canaan.

Now, let's move ahead in time some 400 plus years since Joshua fought the giants of Canaan, and now on the scene is a 16 year old kid named David. This teenager is about to be introduced to one of the giants that remained and his name, of course, was Goliath. David's slaying of the Philistine champion strongman is the best known giant story of all time. Do you ever wonder why David picked up five smooth stones right before he killed Goliath?

"Then he took his staff in his hand; and he chose for himself five smooth stones from the brook, and put them in a shepherd's bag, in a pouch which he had, and his sling was in his hand. And he drew near to the Philistine." 1 Samuel 17: 40[13]

It is a little known fact that Goliath of Gath had four brothers, so maybe David was so confident that he figured after he smote Goliath, his brothers would come after him and he would need to take care of them also. David grew to be a man and he grew to be king of Israel and his armies again fought some Philistine Giants.

"Yet again there was war at Gath, where there was a man of great stature, who had six fingers on each hand and six toes on each foot, twenty-four in number; and he also was born to the giant. So when he defied Israel, Jonathan the son of Shimea, David's brother, killed him." 2 Samuel 21: 20-21[14]

So here we have the slaying of a giant with six fingers on each hand and six toes on each foot, so again we ask the question was this another example of genetic modification being practiced by the giants of the Old Testament? Was there a second incursion of fallen angels that produced another strain of Nephilim? Remember Nimrod from Genesis Chapter 10 and verse 8, we are told that this tyrant began to be a mighty one on the earth. Did Satan give Nimrod special powers as we are told he became a mighty one, which is translated in Hebrew as "gibborim" and that is very similar Hebrew usage as the Genesis chapter 6 description of the Nephilim. There are enough interesting nuggets we can take out of the Scriptures we have explored in this chapter to suggest a supernatural explanation for the giants of the land of Canaan. Through the breeding of fallen angels and women which resulted in giants, or through the wicked practices of sorcery, divination, and child sacrifices the Canaanites could have opened a wicked portal that lead to the demonic manifestation of monstrous creatures set out to destroy God's chosen people?

The despicable culture that flourished in the land of Canaan was repeated again and again by people groups that would follow. The Maya were a people that lived in Central Mexico from 2000 B.C. until they were conquered by the Spanish in the 16th century. Researchers remain baffled by their uncanny ability to navigate and calculate the stars and planets, all this without the benefit of modern astronomy equipment. The famous Mayan calendar which many folks believe ended in 2012 is the anomaly that most people identify with the Maya. So the Maya have in recent years achieved superhero status by many in the world of entertainment and popular culture. It is a distinction that the Maya do not deserve, for these people just like the groups and tribes of the land of Canaan practiced ritualistic child sacrifices to their so called gods. In Mayan sacrifices, the victim's heart was often taken out and displayed while the victim was still alive. Where did this brutality come from? The same demonic influence that the Israelites encountered in the Promised Land was in the world of the Maya and other ancient people groups as well. It is not a stretch at all to expect that such ritualistic horrible acts of violence would result in open manifestations of fallen angels and demons, for indeed, they were the gods the Canaanites and the Mayans really worshiped.

CHAPTER 5
The Smoking Gun to the Nephilim Mystery

From my point of view, one of the best researchers currently looking into the question of the Nephilim is L.A. Marzulli. He has authored several books on the Nephilim mystery, and he is a frequent guest on several popular radio talk shows. Marzulli also keeps a very stringent speaking schedule and maintains a very popular internet web site. In 2013, Marzulli was part of a team of researchers who travelled to Paracas, Peru. The team included respected archaeologist Judd H. Burton, when they arrived at the obscure Paracas History Museum the team discovered over 40 elongated skulls.

As with most discoveries from the ancient past, there is an ongoing controversy surrounding elongated skulls. The conservative or traditional view, (which you will find in many text books) is that these skulls were the result of primitive man's obsession with the practice known as "skull binding". An individual's head was tightly bound with cloth or some other kind of strap throughout their early years. This resulted in the rapid growth of the skull and over time the skull became very large and elongated.

Of the skulls found in Peru, Burton has concluded that four skulls that were found are not "normal". He maintains that the suturing, or the place where the plates which make up the skulls are "stitched" together do not appear as they should. To put it plainly, it does not appear that these four skulls are the result of "skull binding".

The non-traditional view on elongated skulls is that they were possibly extraterrestrials, or perhaps they were the skulls from the ancient Nephilim. The Mayan Serpent gods wore elaborate, elongated skulls and we can even go back as far as the Egyptians of antiquity who worshiped gods that fashioned elongated head dresses. Elongated skulls have been found in Egypt, Mexico, and Peru. Many archaeologists believe that the ruling elite of these ancient peoples were the ones with the elongated skulls, the royal priestly rulers of these people groups.

L.A. Marzulli is having DNA testing done on the skulls that were deemed "not normal", and we await the results with much anticipation. Marzulli and Burton are both Christians and I would encourage the reader to check out both of these men's published writings on the subject of the Nephilim.

Marzulli and Burton believe it is a strong possibility that during the conquest of Canaan by Joshua and the Israelites, some of the giants may have fled to Europe and migrated there. Then they eventually settled in the America's. Believe it or not, bones from extremely large people are a part of history, and dare I say, even a part of American history.

Archaeologist Cyrus Thomas from the Bureau of Ethnology recovered remains suggesting a race of giants in the Ohio River Valley.[1]

In the state of Indiana, archaeologists found a skeleton which measured nine feet and eight inches in length. The skeleton was unearthed while researchers were digging into a burial mound. The skeleton also had a large mica necklace around its neck, this discovery occurred in the year 1879.[2] The giants of Canaan carried spears that weighed upwards of 20 pounds. The biblical narrative records a giant with a spear whose shaft was like a weavers beam (2 Samuel 21: 19).

One of the most amazing discoveries of the remains of extremely large people was the 1936 report of German Paleontologist Larson Kohl who unearthed bones of giants on the shore of Lake Elyasi in Central Africa.[3]

The internet is full of websites which feature photographs of giant remains. But now, it is so easy to forge or alter a photograph, so these websites do not carry very much credibility with mainstream scientists and researchers. Joe Taylor, the curator of the Mount Blanco Fossil Museum in Crosbyton, Texas has in his possession a replica of a huge femur bone which was discovered in southeastern Turkey. There is a photograph of Joe Taylor displaying this replica with the outline of a large man in the background.[4]

Turn of the century mythology and fairy tales certainly are rich with tales of giants. We have the British fairy tale of "Jack and the Beanstalk" where our young hero barely escapes with his life after encountering a blood thirsty giant. In North American folklore, we have the lumberjack figure known as Paul Bunyan who legend says was a giant and a masterful lumberjack of incredible skill. His animal companion was a massive blue ox known as "Babe the Blue Ox" who had great strength. In Gertrude Landa's Jewish Fairy Tales and Legends,[5] we have the story of King Og who survives Noah's flood by riding on the back of a unicorn behind the ark. This is the same giant as the one described in the book of Deuteronomy. There are those who believe some giants survived the Noahic Flood. This way of thinking contradicts God's Word which clearly says that only eight people, that being Noah's family survived the biblical flood. One of the oldest recorded writings we have is the 4000 year old tale called "The Epic of Gilgamesh". In this poem, the main character of Gilgamesh is described as a giant. He is also described as a demigod with superhuman strength. Gilgamesh sounds a lot like a pre-flood Nephilim.

History and mythology being what they are, will we one day in the future with our advanced technology prove that the giants of Canaan actually did escape and branch out in other areas on the planet? Maybe one day a researcher like LA Marzulli or Judd Burton will bring back undeniable proof of the existence of the Nephilim? Being true to the title of this book, let me now present my so called "smoking gun" to the mystery of the Nephilim. My evidence has not been dug up from the ground, and it is not in some remote cave on the Afghanistan border. My evidence is in the obscure book of Amos in the Old Testament of the Bible.

The prophet Amos's ministry involved calling the leaders of Israel to repent. God was a just God and if ancient Israel did not change its course God would administer His justice as only He can in a very mighty way.

In chapter 2 of the book of Amos, God is declaring judgment on Israel. The nation had perverted His Holy name by its pagan worship and actions. In verse 9, God reminds the people through the prophet Amos of what He has already accomplished.

"Yet it was I who destroyed the Amorite before them, Whose height was like the height of the cedars, And he was as strong as the oaks; Yet I destroyed his fruit above And his roots beneath." Amos 2: 9[6]

As we have already studied, God would allow the wicked practices of the Amorites to continue until they had reached their full measure.

Then the Amorites would be executed when their iniquity reached the critical level.

The emphatic statement of God in Amos Chapter 2 and verse 9 is that God declares it was Him who destroyed the previous inhabitants of the land of Canaan. The Israelites under the skillful leadership of Joshua and later David had the sovereign hand of God upon them when their armies defeated the various giant clans of the Old Testament. God describes the height of the Amorites comparing them to the height of cedars. Cedar trees in Lebanon had very imposing trunks and in some cases could attain a height of 70 to 80 feet. God also declares that the Amorite was as strong as the oaks which were known for their strength. God said He destroyed the Amorite's "fruit above and his roots beneath" which means a complete and total destruction. The Amorites were one of the giant clans witnessed by the spies that Moses sent to spy out the land of Canaan. Many Bible commentators look at the bad report the spies brought back to the Israelite camp when they reported seeing giants in the land which made them look like grasshoppers as a slanderous lie. Based on Amos chapter 2, God Himself is declaring the unbelievable height of the Amorites. God is validating the report of the spies! I am not saying that the giants in the land of Canaan were 120 feet tall, but they certainly were not six foot nine inches tall either? Through the prophet Amos, God is declaring that the Amorites were very tall and very strong. I think the passage in Amos hints at the possible supernatural origin of the giants in the land of Canaan. Often conservative minded teachers of the Bible will criticize those of us who see a possible intrusion of fallen angels in the land of Canaan similar to the events in the book of Genesis. If you take the passage in Amos in a straightforward manner then you have to keep yourself open to the possibilities of another satanic intrusion in Canaan just like we had before the flood. And it would certainly appear that the giants in Canaan did not suffer from gigantism which leaves one extremely weak and lethargic. The passage in Amos testifies to their strength.

Here is a summary on what we have covered so far in regards to Genesis chapter 6 and the giant tribes found in the Old Testament:

1. The phrase "sons of God" is from the Hebrew (B'nai Ha Elohim), it is used 8 times in the Old Testament and the context is always divine beings, angels.

2. Genesis Chapter 6: 1-4 is describing the "sons of God" procreating with the daughters of men, these were fallen angels who gave up their heavenly abode to carry out this act.

3. The result of this union between the "sons of God" and the daughters of men were the Nephilim which in Hebrew means "fallen ones". The Nephilim were men of extremely large size and were known for their detestable evil acts against humanity.

4. The motive for the events of Genesis 6 was a satanic intrusion meant to contaminate the human race. Noah was a righteous man; the Scripture indicates that Noah's family was not a part of the activities of the "sons of God". The flood was a judgment of God on the extreme wickedness found on the earth. The main reason for the flood was to stop the procreating of the "sons of God" and daughters of men and also to destroy the result of these unions which were the evil tyrants known as the Nephilim.

5. After the flood, we are introduced to a man named Nimrod who was a "mighty one on the earth". He began the kingdom of Babel. Nimrod is described as a "gibborim" a similar Hebrew phrasing as we have for the Nephilim of Genesis chapter 6. Nimrod it appears was a demonically enhanced individual and he is credited with starting the false religious system known in Scripture in a literal and figurative sense as "Babylon".

6. The book of Enoch, although not part of the Bible, was an important manuscript in the early church. Jude verse 14 quotes from the book of Enoch directly. The book of Enoch speaks of the "sons of God" as "watchers," and these were the angels that left heaven and lusted after the women of the earth in Genesis

chapter 6. The book of Enoch describes the initial place where these fallen angels touched down and that was Mount Hermon in the days of Jared. The book of Enoch also claims that the watchers instructed mankind in the use of charms and magic. The book of Enoch also mentions the Nephilim and tells us that right before the judgment of God through the flood, the Nephilim had become so wicked that they were devouring one another's flesh.

7. We read in Genesis 14:5 that people of extremely large stature were already in the land of Canaan. This timeframe would have been 400 plus years after the flood during the time of Abraham.

8. The giant tribes in the land of Canaan went by various names such as the Amorites, the Anakim, the Emim, the Zuzim, and the Rephaim. The land of Canaan was described as incredibly wicked, with the practices of the occult, the worship of many gods, and the institution of child and infant sacrifices, we know the giants that inhabited the land were inherently evil as well.

9. When Moses sent out 12 spies to survey the land of Canaan they came back with a report that there were giants in the land. Only 2 of the spies Joshua and Caleb wanted to enter the land and fight these giants.

10. When Joshua entered the Promised Land he was instructed to defeat the giants and also wipe out every man, woman, and child of certain tribes. Was this an indication that the land of Canaan had a similar event as the Genesis chapter 6 episode? Was the result a "gene pool issue" in which God would need total extermination of the affected people just like the days before the Noahic Flood?

11. After the defeat of the giant clans of Canaan, Scripture tells us that some still remained outside of the land of Canaan. And it would be an estimated 400 years later that David would defeat the Philistine giant known as Goliath. As king of Israel, David's army would tangle with giants and one giant they killed had six

fingers on each hand and six toes on each foot. Could the wicked giants have been practicing some form of genetic modification or some other supernatural activity?

It is not improbable at all to conclude that the appearance of the Nephilim before the flood and in the land of Canaan after the flood was a satanic strategy designed to contaminate the bloodlines of the human race, and to interrupt God's eternal plan of sending Jesus Christ in the form of a man to pay the penalty for the sins of all of humanity. The Genesis 6 passage clearly says that the Nephilim were on the earth before the flood and also afterwards. The book of Matthew's gospel opens with the genealogy which resulted in the birth of Jesus Christ in human form. The book of Matthew is telling us that Satan's plan did not work.

It has often been said that if you read a difficult or weird passage in the Bible then you need to study it because it is important. In the book of Isaiah, we read these difficult words.

"They are dead, they will not live; They are deceased, they will not rise. Therefore You have punished and destroyed them, And made all their memory to perish." Isaiah 26: 14[7]

The original Hebrew word for "deceased" is the word "Rephaim" and they inhabited the land of Canaan during the conquest by the Israelites, and they were described as giants. If this passage is intended for mankind in general then it contradicts the Bible, for we know that all humans will one day be resurrected (John 5: 28-29). But the Rephaim will not rise in any future resurrection. Could this be because they were not fully human? In the original Hebrew translation, this hard to understand passage suggests that the giant tribes of Canaan were indeed hybrids. Possibly, they were partly celestial and partly human giving the reality of more fallen angel intrusions with the daughters of men.

One of the more common arguments against the fallen angel view of Genesis 6 comes not from a Scriptural perspective, but from a biological one. How could celestial beings that have an entirely different molecular make up procreate with human women? This is a very good question and although I am not an expert in Biology I think a deeper look into Scripture gives us some clues about this. We are told in the book in of Jude that the angels from the Genesis 6 event "did not keep their proper domain". In fact, these angels are guilty of perhaps the most disturbing evil act recorded in the history of man. The Bible scholar Kenneth S. Wuest puts it this way.

"These angels transgressed the limits of their own natures to invade a realm of created beings of a different nature."[8]

In 1 Corinthians 11: 10, the apostle Paul states that a woman should cover her head as a sign of submission to her husband. Then he adds these curious words: and also "because of the angels". Why did Paul throw that phrase in this passage? No one really has been able to explain this with clear insight, but we do know that the fallen angels saw that the daughters of men were beautiful and they lusted after them. There is an old rabbinical tradition that it was the beauty of the women's long hair that enticed the angels of Genesis 6.But as we know, long beautiful hair on a woman entices plenty of just plain human males, so I am speculating on this.

Many also have asked the very good question of why were the Nephilim all men as made plain by the text itself from Genesis 6? Were these unholy unions the result of chromosome problems? Some questions I admit do not seem to have an answer. This we do know: there was a race of superhuman beings called the Nephilim, and they appear to be active both before and after the flood. What about now, and what about the future, does Bible prophecy allude to these creatures known as the Nephilim?

CHAPTER 6

Nephilim and Bible Prophecy

It has been said that approximately one third of the entire biblical narrative deals with prophecy. Some of the Bible's longest books deal with prophecy like Ezekiel, Isaiah, and Daniel. In fact, every book in the Bible has some prophecy in it. One of the major reasons the Bible has survived to the present day when countless political, religious, and morality movements have failed is the fact that the Holy Word of God contains hundreds of fulfilled biblical prophecies.

"Remember the former things of old, For I am God, and there is no other; I am God, and there is none like Me, Declaring the end from the beginning, And from ancient times things that are not yet done, Saying, 'My counsel shall stand, And I will do all My pleasure,' Isaiah 46: 9-10[1]

Only God, who alone knows the end from the beginning could make a statement like that. God can back up that statement with historically fulfilled prophecies.

The Bible declares that Israel would be enslaved in Egypt, but one day God's people would dwell in their own Promised Land. (Genesis 15: 13-16).

The Bible declares that Israel because of their disobedience would be defeated and taken captive by other nations. (Deuteronomy 28: 25, 36-37).

The Jewish people exiled to Babylon would be allowed to return after a 70 year period of time. (Jeremiah 25: 11-12).

The Bible actually names the ruler who would let the Jewish exiles return and rebuild Jerusalem. His name would be Cyrus. Other historical writings call him Cyrus the Great. (Isaiah 44:28).

The Bible declares that not long after Jesus Christ's death, the temple would be destroyed. (Matthew 23: 37- 24: 2).

The Bible declares that most of the original apostles would die for their faith. (John 15: 20) (Luke 11: 49).

Many prophecy teachers and students claim that in the end times, in the years before the return of Jesus Christ we can expect a "return of the Nephilim", just like in the terrible day's right before the Noahic Flood when humanity had become horribly corrupt.

George Hawkins Pember, in his 1876 masterpiece called "Earths Earliest Ages" analyzed the Olivet Discourse recorded in Matthew chapter 24. He concluded that the end times would be like the days of Noah and that one event would mark that time period, and that would be the return of the Nephilim.

"The appearance upon earth of beings from the Principality of the air, and their unlawful intercourse with the human race."[2]

Why did the great George Hawkins Pember and even Bible students today wonder with great curiosity about a possible return of the Nephilim? There are three important biblical passages that fuel this thinking, one from the gospel of Matthew, and the other two from Luke and the prophetic book of Daniel.

Speaking of His return Jesus states this famous passage:

"But of that day and hour no one knows, not even the angels of heaven, but My Father only. But as the days of Noah were, so also will the coming of the Son of Man be." Matthew 24: 36-37[3]

Jesus in the verses that follow goes on to say that people in those days before the flood were living their lives in complete indifference to the coming disaster of the approaching flood. They were eating and drinking, marrying and giving in marriage. In the days that precede the coming of Jesus Christ, most people will have the exact same mindset as the people before the flood of Genesis had. That is the standard commentary for the above passage; however, many prophecy students point out that Christ was saying that the end times would be just like the days of Noah. So you can ask yourself this question, what was different about the days of Noah when being compared to our day? The answer for some would be the appearance of the "sons of God" and the Nephilim from the Genesis chapter 6 drama.

"And as it was in the days of Noah, so it will be also in the days of the Son of Man:" Luke 17: 26[4]

This brings us to a crossroad, for to investigate this further we have to unscramble the many complicated views within Christendom on the subject of eschatology or the end times.

Before we look at the passage in Daniel about a possible return of the Nephilim, let us go the very end of God's Word where we read this.

"Then I saw an angel coming down from heaven, having the key to the bottomless pit and a great chain in his hand. He laid hold of the dragon,

that serpent of old, who is the Devil and Satan, and bound him for a thousand years;" Revelation 20: 1-2[5]

In Christian terminology we know this "thousand year binding of Satan" will occur right before the millennial reign of Jesus Christ, which is spoken of often in Scripture.

"For as the new heavens and the new earth Which I will make shall remain before Me", says the Lord, "So shall your descendants and your name remain. And it shall come to pass That from one New Moon to another, And from one Sabbath to another, All flesh shall come to worship before Me," says the Lord." Isaiah 66: 22-23[6]

It is a eye opening commentary on the Christian church that the most popular view out there is called "amillennialism". This is an allegorical system which was promoted by Origen in the third century A.D. This view holds that there will be no literal, real, it is going to happen reign of Christ here on the earth. This view would take the above passage and simply say that the language is figurative and poetic. The "amillennial" view of prophecy does not take the one thousand years in Revelation chapter 20 in a face value manner. This view believes that one day Christ will come and ultimately we will go into the eternal state. There is no timing of the rapture debates within "amillennialism", for this view does not see such critical texts like Daniel chapter 2 and Daniel chapter 9 in a face value manner. The best way to disprove this thinking is simply to let the Scriptures speak for themselves. For indeed, Christ is one day going to return and set up His kingdom and reign here on earth, we call this the premillennial position, Christ comes before the millennium and then sets up His kingdom. The best way to show this is to go to Daniel chapter 2 and King Nebuchadnezzar's troubling dream which no one including his finest astrologers and sorcerers could explain to him, finally the King turns to the prophet Daniel for help in interpreting the dream.

"Daniel answered in the presence of the king, and said, "The secret which the king has demanded, the wise men, the astrologers, the magicians, and the soothsayers cannot declare to the king. But there is a God in heaven who reveals secrets, and He has made known to King Nebuchadnezzar what will be in the latter days. Your dream, and the visions of your head upon your bed, were these: As for you, O king, thoughts came to your mind while on your bed, about what would come to pass after this; and He who reveals secrets has made known to you what will be. But as for me, this secret has not been revealed to me because I have more wisdom than anyone living, but for our sakes who made known the interpretation to the king, and that you may know the thoughts of your heart. "You, O king, were watching; and behold, a great image! This great image, whose splendor was excellent, stood before you; and its form was awesome. This image's head was of fine gold, its chest and arms of silver, its belly and thighs of bronze, its legs of iron, its feet partly of iron and partly of clay. You watched while a stone was cut out without hands, which struck the image on its feet of iron and clay, and broke them in pieces. Then the iron, the clay, the bronze, the silver, and the gold were crushed together, and became like chaff from the summer threshing floors; the wind carried them away so that no trace of them was found. And the stone that struck the image became a great mountain and filled the whole earth. "This is the dream. Now we will tell the interpretation of it before the king. You, O king, are a king of kings. For the God of heaven has given you a kingdom, power, strength, and glory; and wherever the children of men dwell, or the beasts of the field and the birds of the heaven, He has given them into your hand, and has made you ruler over them all- you are this head of gold. But after you shall arise another kingdom inferior to yours; then another, a third kingdom of bronze, which shall rule over all the earth. And the fourth kingdom shall be as strong as iron, inasmuch as iron breaks in pieces and shatters everything; and like iron that crushes, that kingdom will break in pieces and crush all the others. Whereas you saw the feet and toes, partly of potter's clay and partly of iron, the kingdom shall be divided; yet the strength of the iron shall be in it, just as you

saw the iron mixed with ceramic clay. And as the toes of the feet were partly of iron and partly of clay, so the kingdom shall be partly strong and partly fragile. As you saw iron mixed with ceramic clay, they will mingle with the seed of men; but they will not adhere to one another, just as iron does not mix with clay. And in the days of these kings the God of heaven will set up a kingdom which shall never be destroyed; and the kingdom shall not be left to other people; it shall break in pieces and consume all these kingdoms, and it shall stand forever. Inasmuch as you saw that the stone was cut out of the mountain without hands, and that it broke in pieces the iron, the bronze, the clay, the silver, and the gold- the great God has made known to the king what will come to pass after this. The dream is certain, and its interpretation is sure."
Daniel 2: 27-45[7]

Critical scholars doubt that the book of Daniel could have been written in and around 530 B.C., the accepted timeframe if you take the book at face value. Because of the precision and detail of predicting the rise and fall of kingdoms mentioned in Daniel chapter 2, which did not occur until the second and third centuries. Critic's claim the book of Daniel had to have been written much later because if the book was written in or around 530 B.C. then it certainly validates that God does know the beginning from the end, which of course, He does.

The world's greatest history lesson given well in advance of the actual fulfillment of the rise of these kingdoms is what we are dealing with in Daniel chapter 2. Daniel explains to King Nebuchadnezzar that "you are this head of gold". Babylon ruled the known world from 626 B.C until 539 B.C. Next, we have the chest and arms of silver and recorded history verifies that Medo-Persia was the empire that followed Babylon. The belly and thighs of bronze was Greece, and then the fourth empire which will "crush all the others" is Rome symbolized by the legs of iron. The ten toes described as partly of iron and partly of clay are generally understood by prophecy students as a future revived Roman Empire of the last days, or to put it simply, the ten toes will represent the kingdom of the Antichrist. The same empires are mentioned again in Daniel chapter 7 where they are represented as beasts. Daniel chapter 7 mentions ten horns that come from the fourth beast which was a terrifying and frightening beast. In the book of Revelation, we read this:

"The ten horns which you saw are ten kings who have received no kingdom as yet, but they receive authority for one hour as kings with the beast." Revelation 17: 12[8]

The Bible details a futuristic vision of 10 kingdoms coming together with "the beast" who in Revelation is the Antichrist and his kingdom.

Of course, the stone from Daniel chapter 2 is a great Old Testament reference to the second coming of Jesus Christ. Please notice that the stone strikes the feet of the image which really fits perfectly because Jesus Christ will one day return at this yet future time in history to reclaim the earth for His Father in heaven, and to defeat the beast or Antichrist and Satan.

After the stone strikes the image a great mountain fills the whole earth, and this represents the millennial kingdom on the earth recreated by God Himself.

In Daniel chapter 2 and verse 43, we see the iron is mixed with ceramic clay and then the passage says that "they" will mingle with the seed of men. Those who ponder a possible return of the Nephilim speculate on who "they" are, and why are they mingling with the seed of men. Is this a reference to some kind of genetic tampering with the human race during the last days similar to the world conditions prior to the great flood? That would certainly add a little more insight to the words of Jesus warning that the day's right before His return would be just like the days of Noah.

Now, let's narrow our study of eschatology to the time of the end of the age. The reader has no doubt heard many preachers and evangelists speak of a future seven year period that will mark earth's last days. Where do the Scriptures teach that and how can we understand it? If Daniel chapter 2 was an amazing prophecy, then the seventy week prophecy of Daniel chapter nine cannot be far behind.

This prophecy has been called the backbone of prophetic interpretation, and I feel that it is absolutely that important. But as with most Scriptures that deal with prophecy, there are various interpretations of Daniel's 70 weeks, so some have called it ultimately unknowable. I do not think God meant for that to be true, and I know and we will see that Jesus Christ did not think the 70 week prophecy was unable to be understood.

Daniel is in deep prayer for his people, that being Israel, and he is paid a visit by the angel Gabriel who tells Daniel that he is greatly beloved. He is about to be given a vision of great understanding, the 70 week prophecy begins with these words.

"Seventy weeks are determined For your people and for your holy city, To finish the transgression, To make an end of sins, To make reconciliation for iniquity, To bring in everlasting righteousness, To seal up vision and prophecy, And to anoint the Most Holy." Daniel 9: 24[9]

In the Hebrew language, "Seventy weeks" can refer to days, weeks, or years. We can say that the "Seventy weeks" in Daniel's prophecy refers to seventy time periods of seven years each for a complete total of 490 prophetic years. This will become clear to the reader as we go further into this prophecy and compare Scripture with Scripture. So this specific prophecy is for Daniel's people (Israel) and for their holy city (Jerusalem). When this prophecy is over Daniel's people will have finished their transgression, and made an end of sins.

Wow! This is getting interesting, is it not. They will have produced reconciliation for their iniquity, and everlasting righteousness will be brought in. Vision and prophecy will be sealed up and the Most Holy will be anointed. Gabriel tells Daniel that Israel and their holy city of Jerusalem will experience 490 more years of persecution and domination before they will have atoned for their sin of rejecting God. When this seventy week prophecy is finished then everlasting righteousness will come and the Most Holy (Jesus Christ) will be anointed.

"Know therefore and understand, That from the going forth of the command To restore and build Jerusalem Until Messiah the Prince, There shall be seven weeks and sixty-two weeks; The street shall be built again, and the wall, Even in troublesome times." Daniel 9: 25[10]

The command to restore and rebuild Jerusalem was actually given by Artaxerxes Longimanus in 445 B.C. (Nehemiah 2:5), when the Jewish exiles began rebuilding Jerusalem which was destroyed by Babylon. So that is the date of the beginning of this amazing prophecy. There would be seven weeks and sixty-two weeks until Messiah the Prince. In the context of this prophecy, that would add up to 483 prophetic years from the rebuilding of Jerusalem until Messiah the Prince. Investigator Sir Robert Anderson wrote a book in the 1800's called "The Coming Prince". In his book, Anderson calculated the time from 445 B.C. until Palm Sunday when Christ appeared in Jerusalem shortly before His execution as being exactly 483 prophetic years of 360 days each according to the Jewish calendar. My friend, how incredible is that, but this most important prophecy in the Bible is still not finished.

"And after the sixty-two weeks Messiah shall be cut off, but not for Himself; And the people of the prince who is to come Shall destroy the city and the sanctuary. The end of it shall be with a flood, And till the end of the war desolations are determined." Daniel 9: 26[11]

The reference of Messiah being cut off is the crucifixion of Jesus Christ. The people of the prince who is to come finds its historical and prophetic fulfillment in Rome. In 70 A.D., the Roman tyrant Titus and his Roman legions began the horrific destruction of Jerusalem, and this event began the scattering of the Jewish people which was foretold in Scripture. The crucifixion of Jesus and then the destruction of Jerusalem and the sanctuary by the Romans, but who is this prince who is to come from verse 26?

"Then he shall confirm a covenant with many for one week; But in the middle of the week He shall bring an end to sacrifice and offering. And on the wing of abominations shall be one who makes desolate, Even until the consummation, which is determined, Is poured out on the desolate."
Daniel 9: 27[12]

He (the prince who is to come) from verse 26 will confirm a covenant for one week (seven years). At the halfway point of this seven year period we see an end to sacrifice and offering and finally the one who is responsible for the desolations is made desolate. The (prince who is to come) is known in Scripture as Antichrist, and there is a long period of time between verse 26 and verse 27 which we are still in as I write this book. A fair question would be why in this seventy week prophecy should we believe that the entire events of the prophecy unfold in succession, and then the last seven year period from verse 27 is still a future event? What right do I or anyone else have in making that claim? Fortunately, when we compare Scripture with Scripture our eyes are opened to this truth.

"Now, brethren, concerning the coming of our Lord Jesus Christ and our gathering together to Him, we ask you, not to be soon shaken in mind or troubled, either by spirit or by word or by letter, as if from us, as though the day of Christ had come. Let no one deceive you by any means; for that Day will not come unless the falling away comes first, and the man of sin is revealed, the son of perdition, who opposes and exalts himself above

all that is called God or that is worshiped, so that he sits as God in the temple of God, showing himself that he is God." 2 Thessalonians 2: 1-4[13]

These words from the apostle Paul when compared to Daniel 9:27 show why many prophecy students expect another Jewish temple will be built in the last days. This "man of sin" will claim to be God when he profanes the temple and demands worship. Many scholars point to the pagan ruler Antiochus Epiphanes who erected an altar to the god Zeus in the temple in Jerusalem in 168 B.C. as a possible fulfillment to Paul's words. But this letter of Paul's was concerning the second coming of Jesus Christ. This "man of sin" sitting in the temple and claiming to be God will happen as a precursor to the return of Jesus. In the Olivet Discourse, Jesus Christ Himself puts the 70th week in the future!

"Therefore when you see the 'abomination of desolation,' spoken of by Daniel the prophet, standing in the holy place" (whoever reads, let him understand)," Matthew 24: 15[14]

The Olivet Discourse includes the second coming of Jesus Christ. Just like Paul would later write, we see the Antichrist of the last days during the last week of Daniel's prophecy demanding worship in the temple, or something similar during that last seven year period. There are timeframe references in the prophetic books of Daniel and Revelation that can only apply to the 70th week of Daniel.

"Then I heard the man clothed in linen, who was above the waters of the river, when he held up his right hand and his left hand to heaven, and swore by Him who lives forever, that it shall be for a time, times, and half a time; and when the power of the holy people has been completely shattered, all these things shall be finished." Daniel 12: 7[15]

Time, times, and half a time is understood to be a period of three and one-half years, which would be the last half of the seven year period of Daniel's prophecy. Time equals one year, times equals two years, and half a time equals a half a year, so we have three and one half years or half of the 70th week of Daniel, the last half.

"Then the woman fled into the wilderness, where she has a place prepared by God, that they should feed her there one thousand two hundred and sixty days." Revelation 12: 6[16]

In the symbolic language of Revelation, the woman that flees into the wilderness is Israel, and the one thousand two hundred and sixty days or 42 months (Revelation 11:2), correspond to the last half of the final week (7 years) from Daniel's famous prophecy(42 months x 30 days = 1260 days). We can even go further in investigating this last seven year period. If we go to Matthew chapter 24, Jesus is having a conversation with His disciples about the events that would unfold before He returned. If we compare Matthew chapter 24 with the apocalyptic language of Jesus Christ in Revelation chapter 6, we begin to see some startling similarities, and we can really get a picture of the great tribulation still yet future.

The second coming of Christ in relation to the last seven year period of Daniel's prophecy (Daniel's 70th week) is probably the most debated prophecy matter for premillennial believers. We have the popular pretribulation theory that puts the coming of Christ or rapture before the 70th week of Daniel begins. The highly successful "Left Behind" series of books promoted a pretribulational rapture. The other positions are the midtribulational rapture which is at the mid-point of Daniel's 70th week, and the posttribulational position which puts the coming of Christ at the end of Daniel's 70th week. A comparison of Matthew chapter 24 and Revelation chapter 6 will show you where the biblical evidence rests on the rapture debate.

"For the Lord Himself will descend from heaven with a shout, with the voice of an archangel, and with the trumpet of God. And the dead in

Christ will rise first. Then we who are alive and remain shall be caught up together with them in the clouds to meet the Lord in the air. And thus we shall always be with the Lord. Therefore comfort one another with these words." 1 Thessalonians 4: 16-17[17]

The above words of the Apostle Paul describe the coming of Christ. When does this happen in relation to the 70th week of Daniel? In Matthew chapter 24, the disciples ask Jesus what will be the sign of your coming and of the end of the age? Jesus first response is to not be deceived.

"For many will come in My name, saying 'I am the Christ', and will deceive many." Matthew 24: 5[18]

We have many false teachers on the scene today, but when the 70th week of Daniel commences we will see many arise who will claim to be the Messiah, and no doubt false signs and miracles will ensue.

Now keep in mind that in Matthew chapter 24 Jesus is having a simple conversation with some of his closest followers. In the book of Revelation, beginning with the seal judgments, we have the symbolic description of these same conditions and events of the 70th Week of Daniel. So in fact, Matthew chapter 24 and Revelation chapter 6 should be describing the same events, which as we will see they are.

"Now I saw when the Lamb opened one of the seals; and I heard one of the four living creatures saying with a voice like thunder, "Come and see". And I looked, and behold, a white horse. He who sat on it had a bow; and a crown was given to him, and he went out conquering and to conquer." Revelation 6: 1-2[19]

In the book of Revelation, we have portrayed two riders on a white horse, and the rider in chapter 19 is called faithful and true and that rider is Jesus Christ. The rider in the Revelation 6 passage is the ultimate false christ, that being the Antichrist. The 70ᵗʰ week opens with this rider going out to conquer by deception.

"And you will hear of wars and rumors of wars. See that you are not troubled; for all these things must come to pass, but the end is not yet. For nation will rise against nation, and kingdom against kingdom. And there will be famines, pestilences, and earthquakes in various places. All these are the beginning of sorrows." Matthew 24: 6-8[20]

Jesus in the Olivet Discourse mentions wars and rumors of wars, and in Revelation chapter 6 and verses 3 and 4 we see the rider on the red horse, he is given a sword and he conquers through war. Jesus in Matthew 24 mentions famines, and in Revelation chapter 6 and verses 5 and 6 we have the rider on the black horse who is given a scale to measure the food supply. This rider brings famine. Jesus mentions pestilences, and at the fourth seal we have the rider in Revelation 6 and verses 7 and 8 described as a rider on a pale horse who brings death, hunger, and pestilences.

"Then they will deliver you up to tribulation and kill you, and you will be hated by all nations for My name's sake." Matthew 24: 9[21]

Jesus predicts that Christians will be openly opposed and killed during this period. In Revelation chapter 6 and verses 9 through 11, we have the same thing foretold by Christ.

"When He opened the fifth seal, I saw under the altar the souls of those who had been slain for the word of God and for the testimony which they held. And they cried with a loud voice, saying, "How long, O Lord, holy and true, until You judge and avenge our blood on those who dwell on the earth?" Then a white robe was given to each of them; and it was said to them that they should rest a little while longer, until both the number of their fellow servants and their brethren, who would be killed as they were, was completed." Revelation 6: 9-11[22]

Imagine the sadness and even comfort that the apostle John must have had on the island of Patmos when he saw and recorded this vision of end time events. We know John and his friends were undergoing terrible persecution by the Romans during the time he wrote the book of Revelation. The prophetic comparison of Matthew 24 and Revelation 6 has been spot on to this point, and it should be for God's Word does not contradict itself, now we arrive at the return of Jesus Christ.

"Immediately after the tribulation of those days the sun will be darkened, and the moon will not give its light; the stars will fall from heaven, and the powers of the heavens will be shaken. Then the sign of the Son of Man will appear in heaven, and then all the tribes of the earth will mourn, and they will see the Son of Man coming on the clouds of heaven with power and great glory." Matthew 24: 29-30[23]

Jesus explains that the "sign" of the sun being darkened and the moon not giving its light will precede His return, along with the stars falling from heaven. In a perfect match we read this in Revelation chapter 6.

"I looked when He opened the sixth seal, and behold, there was a great earthquake; and the sun became black as sackcloth of hair, and the moon became like blood. And the stars of heaven fell to the earth, as a fig tree drops its late figs when it is shaken by a mighty wind." Revelation 6: 12-13[24]

The sixth seal of Revelation announces the arrival of God's wrath, and these cosmic disturbances in the sun, moon, and stars precede both God's wrath and the return of Jesus. When Jesus returns the dead in Christ and all those who remain alive will be caught up to meet Christ in the clouds, and then for those left, the wrath of God begins. Old Testament prophecy calls this time period the "Day of the Lord" and in perfect harmony of God's prophetic revelation, the Day of the Lord is preceded by cosmic disturbances.

"Behold, the day of the Lord comes, Cruel, with both wrath and fierce anger, To lay the land desolate; And He will destroy its sinners from it. For the stars of heaven and their constellations Will not give their light; The sun will be darkened in its going forth, And the moon will not cause its light to shine." Isaiah 13: 9-10[25]

"Multitudes, multitudes in the valley of decision! For the day of the Lord is near in the valley of decision. The sun and moon will grow dark, And the stars will diminish their brightness." Joel 3: 14-15[26]

This author does not believe in date setting or predicting when Jesus Christ will return. But in holding to taking Scripture at face value, we see the coming of Christ after the midpoint of Daniel's 70th Week and after the sixth seal of Revelation chapter 6. There will be signs in the sun, moon, and stars that signal both the return of Christ for His elect and the "Day of the Lord" or God's wrath which believers will not experience.

The Olivet Discourse and the seal judgments of Revelation chapter 6 describe deception, war, famines, disease, earthquakes, and pestilences and all of these conditions exist now at present day. They will increase as the 70th week of Daniel comes closer and then begins. The book of Revelation then describes the Trumpet and Bowl judgments which are the wrath of God. These judgments are supernatural judgments and in the Revelation they are carried out by angels.

The most incredible and hard to believe of the trumpet judgments is the fifth trumpet judgment in which demon possessed locusts arise out of a bottomless pit, and begin tormenting men for five months. The king of this demonic army is then described.

"And they had as king over them the angel of the bottomless pit, whose name in Hebrew is Abaddon, but in Greek he has the name Apollyon." Revelation 9: 11[27]

Some biblical scholars see this king, or Abaddon, or Apollyon, as Satan himself. There is also speculation that these demonic locusts being set free from their prison during the trumpet judgments could be the "angels that sinned" in the days of Noah. These angels were imprisoned (2 Peter 2: 4-5) for their disobedience. The name Apollyon in the Greek usage of the word means "Destroyer or Destruction", and some even speculate that the word is closely linked to the Greek god known as Apollo. So perhaps this "angel of the bottomless pit" could even be the Antichrist. Or better yet, maybe the angel is a Nephilim? There is a view that says the "sons of God" and their offspring the Nephilim were the same type of entities, but that would contradict Scripture.

So our journey into biblical prophecy has not produced a conclusive Scripture that states that the pre flood giants of antiquity will return during the last days, but some will point to this passage in the book of Isaiah.

"The burden against Babylon which Isaiah the son of Amoz saw. Lift up a banner on the high mountain, Raise your voice to them; Wave your hand, that they may enter the gates of the nobles. I have commanded My sanctified ones; I have also called My mighty ones for My anger- Those who rejoice in My exaltation." Isaiah 13: 1-3[28]

The term "mighty ones" is the Hebrew word "gibborim" and it is the same term used to describe the giants of Genesis chapter 6. In this lament against Babylon could the prophet be warning of Nephilim coming to the land of Babylon, and could this return be in the 70th Week of Daniel? Time will tell.

One thing is for certain, the demonic realm and fallen angels have been active since the dawn of human existence. There is no reason not to believe, and a straightforward reading of Scripture will inform us that manifestations of fallen angels, and the demonic will continue to increase as history unfolds before us.

"For they are spirits of demons, performing signs, which go out to the kings of the earth and of the whole world, to gather them to the battle of that great day of God Almighty." Revelation 16: 14[29]

"Now the Spirit expressly says that in latter times some will depart from the faith, giving heed to deceiving spirits and doctrines of demons." 1 Timothy 4: 1[30]

Filtering history with the lens of Scripture shows these above verses to be right on the money.

Joseph Smith was visited by an "angel" and those visits inspired the early forming of Mormonism.

Many new age groups speak of channeling and speaking to manifesting spirits and extraterrestrials.

Nazi Germany under the demonic leadership of Adolf Hitler persecuted the Jewish people and lasted for twelve years. At the heart of the Nazi's was their obsession with the occult, and Hitler wanted to create a new species of human being and usher in a "thousand year Reich".

The world of the occult and false religion began with Nimrod and the tower of Babel, and it continued into the land of Canaan, then into the culture of many ancient people groups like the Mayans. In the middle ages, people spoke of encountering incubus and demons and today we have people speaking of encountering ghosts, shadow people, and aliens. All this can be put under one deceptive umbrella, we call it the "realm of the demonic" and it is a place to avoid.

Ultimately, the returning Jesus Christ will destroy this demonic realm once and for all. The Greek New Testament word for the second coming of Christ is the phrase "parousia", and it implies an event with many activities associated with it. At the first "parousia" of Christ we saw His birth, His ministry, His death, His resurrection, and His ascension into Heaven. At His second "parousia" we will see the rapture (1 Thessalonians 4:15), God's wrath on the wicked that remain, the remnant from Israel receiving salvation (Romans 11:25-26), God reclaiming control of the earth, and the destruction of Antichrist and his army at Armageddon. The view of Christ's return that has the most biblical evidence is the pre-wrath view, and that is how I presented this chapter. We can all agree that the return of Jesus Christ is the ultimate absolute of human history, and that one sweet day it is going to happen. Go tell it on the mountain as the old hymn says.

CHAPTER 7

Nephilim and the UFO Phenomenon

In recent space news that you may have missed, the space probe known as Voyager 1 recently celebrated a pretty major milestone. On or around August 25, 2012, NASA scientists have strong evidence that the probe has become the first man-made object to leave our solar system. Voyager 1 is the first human-made object to depart the heliosphere, which is the magnetic boundary separating our sun and the planets from the rest of the galaxy. Voyager 1 was launched in 1977; it is travelling at a speed of 38,000 miles per hour. It is just now starting to enter the fringes of interstellar space, and Voyager 1 will fly near its next star in about 40,000 years according to NASA scientists. Allow me to emphasize the obvious; the observable universe is pretty darn big!

Secular scientists estimate the universe is about thirteen and a half billion years old, and some ninety billion light-years across. On a crisp, clear night about three thousand stars can be visible from earth. Scientists speculate that there are around 125 billion galaxies, and each galaxy is projected to have billions of stars. A galaxy is a massive cluster of stars held together by gravity which moves as a unit. The galaxy we earthlings call our own is called the Milky Way, and it is a spiral galaxy with billions of stars. The Milky Way's neighbor galaxy is called Andromeda, and it is a mere two and a half million light-years away from us.

We have come a long, long, way since the days of Galileo and his audacity for claiming that the earth was not the center of the universe, or even the center of our solar system. The last 100 years have been mind boggling in the world of cosmology and space exploration, and many see the discoveries that are just before us as possibly the death blows for the Bible, and traditional Christian doctrines and our view of God and Jesus Christ. The inspiration of Scripture will soon all need to be revised. In the year 1929, which was not that long ago, astronomer Edwin Hubble published a landmark paper which spawned from his research. Edwin Hubble's paper was about the rate of expansion of the universe, and this overturned the long held belief by scientists that the universe was mostly unchanging, empty, and predictable. The universe is constantly expanding, so does that mean it is infinite and has no end? Many theories have arisen since Hubble's major discovery. Are there multiverses, could our universe just be one of many in a great cosmic bubble? How about parallel universes and world's that could be just a wormhole away from us in some alternate reality, or another dimension of time, space, and matter? I can hear the words of Rod Serling, welcome to the Twilight Zone.

In 2009, NASA launched the Kepler space telescope and its mission was to search the Milky Way galaxy for earth sized planets in the most habitable places of our solar system. The telescopes main instrument was called a photometer which monitors the brightness in a fixed field of view. When an exoplanet crosses in front of its host star the photometer measures the dimming effect. If you can imagine a bug passing in front of your cars headlight then you sort of get the picture. The data is analyzed and the discovery of another planet is made. As of February 2014, Kepler had discovered 961 confirmed exoplanets in some 76 stellar systems and a high number of other planet candidates waiting to be confirmed.

With this data to consider secular scientists can now boldly proclaim that our earth is really not that special at all, and there are most likely thousands upon thousands of planets similar to ours in the ever expanding universe. So then the next step of educated speculation is taken, there must be life out there in the cosmos, for if life evolved here on earth, and as we are discovering there is nothing special about earth. Then life has to be elsewhere in the universe, it had to evolve on other planets also. The increasingly popular theory of Panspermia is often cited. Panspermia is the belief that microorganisms or other compounds from outer space are responsible for starting life on earth. Panspermia could also occur in other places in the vast universe if the conditions in the atmosphere are suitable for life. Many believe what jump started Panspermia was possibly an asteroid that crashed on earth and the microorganisms attached to the asteroid began the process of life evolving on planet earth. The brilliant astrophysicist Neil DeGrasse Tyson sums up the scientific communities line of reasoning on possible alien life with a profound comment from his excellent book, "Death By Black Hole". Neil DeGrasse Tyson makes the very compelling argument in his book that if our solar system is not all that unusual, and there are so many planets in the universe, so many that they outnumber the sum of all sounds ever spoken by every human being that has ever lived. He goes on to conclude that speaking of earth as the only planet with life would be awfully bigheaded of us.[1] Creationists, and this author is one of them, wonder about the claim that the universe is some thirteen and a half billion years old. The biblical account would seem to indicate a much younger earth, and the following observations cannot be ignored.

The solar system earth resides in extends about two-thirds of the way towards the edge of the Milky Way, so our planet is least likely to suffer collisions with other stars. Most of the stars in the spiral Milky Way galaxy are in the center. There are fewer stars near us which amounts to fewer chances of cosmic problems like a star going supernova which would flood the earth with deadly radiation.

The earth's huge moon also protects us from the many asteroids that enter our neighborhood of the solar system. There is a reason the surface of the moon looks like shredded cheese, our abnormally large moon's gravitational pull has sucked in many asteroids that otherwise would have been crashing into earth.

Our sun has been placed at just the perfect place within the galaxy to keep the temperatures and our atmosphere at just the right levels, and our energy and fresh water levels are unusually stable.

The rest of the planets in our solar system do not even come close to the stability we find here on planet earth. On Mercury, temperatures range from 800 degrees Fahrenheit to -298 degrees Fahrenheit. The temperatures on Venus can reach 931 degrees Fahrenheit, and Jupiter which is the largest planet in our solar system has incredible storms almost every day. The large red spot on Jupiter is actually a huge hurricane.

Earth may be just a small and rocky obscure planet in our vast universe. But to declare that it is not a special place would be premature and incorrect and would contradict what God's Holy Word says about the earth.

"The heaven, even the heavens, are the Lord's; But the earth He has given to the children of men." Psalm 115: 16[2]

Even with the many new exoplanets we are discovering, we are still at this point unable to peer into the atmospheres of these newly discovered worlds. Most scientists will admit that most of the new planets being discovered are gas giants similar to the planet Jupiter in our solar system. Earth is a special place, and you can believe the amazing cosmic events that secured the safety we enjoy on this planet as mere lucky circumstances, or you can know that God created our planet for us, and His handiwork cannot be denied.

In Psalm 136, we are told that God "laid out the earth above the waters" and God made the moon and stars to rule by night. Often critics of the Bible describe Scripture as being too simplistic and therefore it cannot be trusted in the same way as Science. The Bible was never meant to be a scientific manual of any kind. The Scriptures were written in the context and the culture of the people who were inspired to write it. The best way a first century Israelite could describe the night sky would be to proclaim that God "hung" the stars in the sky, and that does not imply that God has no knowledge of black holes, quasars, and supernovas. God created all that stuff too and in our postmodern world where we are boldly going where no man has gone before it is still not an incorrect statement to say that it was God who "hung" the stars in the sky.

Considering the possibility of life on other planets not only divides the secular world, but it also leads to different thoughts and ideas from the Christian world. A good broad measuring stick on this debate would be to characterize it in the following manner. The more "liberal" thinking Christians find little difficulty in the concept of aliens being out there in the cosmos. If God placed life on earth then He could place it elsewhere if He so wished. The "conservative" minded Christian would find the idea of extraterrestrials as a threat to biblical Christianity. The discovery of extraterrestrials would confirm the theory of evolution. The discovery of technologically superior extraterrestrials would undermine the authority of Scripture which claims that mankind is God's crowning achievement in the universe. This debate has continued since the days of the Enlightenment which weakened so many Protestant principles. Thomas Paine wrote this in his book called "The Age of Reason":

"Are we to suppose that every world in the boundless creation had an Eve, an apple, a serpent and a redeemer? In this case the person who is irreverently called the Son of God, and sometimes God himself, would have nothing else to do than to travel from world to world, in an endless succession of deaths, with scarcely a momentary interval of life."[3]

On answering the question of why did God create such a vast universe many will say, what is "big" to God? But it is a logical and fair question to ask, for if the only heart beating life forms in the universe are found here on this little planet we call earth then there is a lot of "empty space" out there.

The Bible does not in so many words give a direct answer to the question of extraterrestrial life on other planets. I would define extraterrestrial in this case as an intelligent life form on another planet who lives with others and has a life expectancy similar to ours. To say this a little more to the point, is there a life form on another world somewhere who gets up every morning and struggles to make it to work on time, eats way to much junk food, does not understand why his children act the way they do, and spends way to much of his time in needless arguments with his wife, which he knows beforehand will not end well for him? The Scriptures do not affirm such a creature other than the ones we find here on earth.

The Bible states that the entire creation travails and groans under the weight of sin (Romans 8:18-22). The results of what happened in the Garden of Eden were universal. Every person born on this planet has inherited the Adamic curse, and when Christ appeared on earth He was the sinless substitute to accept the punishment we all deserve. Christ's death on Calvary was for human beings, not for Vulcan's and little gray aliens. The Scriptures call Jesus "the last Adam," for there really was a first Adam who messed things up for us earthlings.

It is a fair statement that the Bible implies that life the way we know it to be can only be found here on earth. God could have created life elsewhere, for it is within His Sovereignty to do what He wishes. The Bible declares that the entire universe has suffered the effects of the revolt by Satan and the subsequent fall of man. But God could place life elsewhere and use that life for reasons only known to Him, the Bible does not seem to say that but we cannot rule it out.

"For by Him all things were created that are in heaven and that are on earth, visible and invisible, whether thrones or dominions or principalities or powers. All things were created through Him and for Him." Colossians 1: 16[4]

The Bible does mention other (celestial) life, and that life is described as "the Heavenly Host" for it is the realm of the divine.If we are honest with ourselves, it is a realm that we know very little about and it is the world of angels.

No Christian should ever refer to this vast universe we now live in as mere "empty space". It was a celestial creature who said in Isaiah chapter 14, "I will exalt my throne above the stars of God." It was this same celestial creature (Satan) who is spoken of in Ezekiel chapter 28 as walking among the fiery stones (stars and planets). And we are told in the New Testament book of Ephesians that Satan is "the prince of the power of the air".

There is life in the universe other than mankind and that life visited this planet ages ago when the "sons of God" came from somewhere else and began the drama we have studied from Genesis chapter six. Of course, any type of discussion on the possibilities of extraterrestrial life is not complete without diving into the subject of UFOs.

The UFO Phenomenon and all the many subsets that go along with it is something I am quite familiar with. My personal fascination with UFOs began when I was in High School. I read a book by J. Allen Hynek which was in my school's library. In recent years, I have devoted a great deal of my free time looking into UFO sightings as a Field Investigator with the highly respected civilian organization group known as MUFON, which stands for the Mutual UFO Network. MUFON's mission is the scientific study of UFOs for the benefit of mankind. Volunteers and investigators are in all 50 states and abroad as well. MUFON operates an integral website and public reports of unidentified aerial phenomena are investigated as objectively as possible. In the wacky world of UFOs, MUFON has usually stood out as an objective source for reporting strange objects and phenomena seen in the skies.

The modern UFO phenomenon began in World War II when over the skies of Germany appeared many unknown glowing objects; the American pilots nicknamed these objects as "Foo Fighters". Seeing and reporting a strange sight in the sky is not a modern occurrence, in fact, it has been with mankind since the dawn of time. In Egyptian mythology, their sun god known as Ra was reported to have flown on a "celestial boat", and the Egyptian deity called Horus is said to have flown on a winged disc of many colors.

At the conclusion of World War II, sightings of UFOs really skyrocketed and an iconic sighting took place on June 24, 1947. Kenneth Arnold, a private pilot, was flying near Mount Rainier in Washington State when he reported observing nine disc shaped objects against the snow covered peaks of Mount Rainier. Kenneth Arnold described what he saw as "like saucers being skipped across water." With the media attention the Arnold sighting received, the phrase stuck and that is how we got the term "flying saucer". The Roswell Incident soon followed and as the 1950's began reports of

Unidentified Flying Objects became commonplace. It was the drama of the cold war and tensions between the United States and the Soviet Union were on the rise. The American military was secretly working on the development of many secret craft even craft that was disc-shaped. The United States during this period launched three organizations that evaluated aerial phenomena. They were known as Project Sign and Project Grudge and the most famous organization known as Project Blue Book, which was operated by the United States Air Force. Project Blue Book operated throughout the 1950's until 1969 when it was concluded that there was no evidence that Unidentified Flying Objects were a threat to the national security of the United States. Project Blue Book ended with 10, 147 sightings recorded.

Which brings us to a very important conclusion regarding unidentified aerial phenomena, and that is that most of the strange stuff we see in the night sky can be explained with proper and educated investigation.

Bright stars and planets account for a large portion of UFO reports. Bright stars or planets seem very large when they are rising or setting. Because of the dispersion of light as it travels through our atmosphere the shape of stars or planets can appear bizarre and flash with blue, red, and green colors. The planet Venus when it is low on the horizon accounts for a lot of UFO sightings.

Meteors, which are pieces of matter burning up in our atmosphere, are often reported as UFOs. They are commonly called "shooting stars" although they have nothing to do with stars at all. The most brilliant meteors are called "fireballs" or "bolides". They can appear as extremely large objects in the sky and exhibit bright colors of white, green, blue, yellow, and red. Some leave a luminous trial behind them and when they fragment or break up they can even appear to go sideways in the sky.

Comets, the moon, ball lighting, marsh gas, are other natural phenomena that often get reported as UFOs. Flares, weather balloons, drones, and Chinese fire lanterns are some manmade objects that can be reported as UFOs.

Military aircraft are often mistaken for UFOs and that brings me to an often overlooked observation on the modern UFO phenomenon. Many of the objects being reported are prototypes of secret military craft, and in many cases the military is quite comfortable with the objects they are testing being reported as UFOs. The F-117 stealth aircraft and the strange looking B2 stealth bomber were no doubt reported as UFOs during the 1970's and 1980's. The F-117A is a craft that is triangular shaped which matched the shape of many UFO descriptions.

A fascinating UFO wave that is extremely well documented is the "Belgian Triangle" wave which occurred over a seven month period beginning in November of 1989. Reports of strange moving triangular vehicles flooded the small country of Belgium. Many speculated that the sightings were the stealth F-117A which was known to operate out of USAF bases in eastern England. The majority of reports were of hovering low altitude triangular craft and that would eliminate the F-117A which is not able to hover silently. The wave over Belgium is still unsolved to this day, and remains a UFO mystery.

A vehicle that does have the ability to hover is the helicopter, and many UFO reports are military or civilian helicopters. Helicopters are rectangular, egg shaped, or triangular vehicles which have the ability to hover in one place for long periods of time. The flight maneuverability of helicopters can appear quite spectacular at night, and helicopters can display sudden accelerations and sharp turns in the sky. When a pilot turns off the navigation lights at night, it can appear that the vehicle has disappeared. Many military helicopters have special mufflers which can make them almost silent especially if they are being flown downwind.

From my perspective, as an investigator, the bulk of explained sightings can be attributed to meteors being observed or military training exercises. It is a general rule of thumb among the organizations that research UFOs that approximately 95 percent of all sightings reported from civilians can be explained with proper investigation. That would leave us with 5 percent of reports that are left unexplained after investigation. One of the last sightings I worked on was a report of strange lights seen in the Raleigh/Durham area of North Carolina. Calls flooded into the 911 dispatchers as the strange lights were observed over a stretch of interstate highway and other locations too. The next day the news reported that the lights were night time helicopters involved in a military training exercise. But a couple of witnesses from Johnston County, North Carolina spoke to me about a vehicle they viewed that same night that they could not explain. The object was a huge airship type craft which they only were able to see the back side of. The craft had a row of three white lights on the back side and the color of the object was charcoal grey. After I interviewed the witnesses, I went back and found a similar sighting of a large charcoal grey craft hovering silently in the night sky from Kill Devil Hills, North Carolina a few months prior to the Johnston County sighting. In my mind, this was probably a prototype of a new airship the military is working on.

The military has a name for these aerial vehicles (long-endurance multi-intelligence vehicle) or LEMV. These vehicles have been in the skies quite often since 2009. Some of these airships are being constructed with a similar design to the many triangular UFOs that have been reported since 2009. High altitude airships are a big part of the new wave of stealth technology being employed by private contractors and the military. The infamous stealth blimp goes back to reports that began in earnest in 1999. Elizabeth City, North

Carolina is a location where this vehicle was worked on. Even if most UFO reports can be explained it is still a fascinating subject to study. Actually, you will find that patents related to triangular shaped aircraft go back as far as the 1920's. Lockheed Martin has a huge bulky craft called the "skytug", and the United States has realized the many benefits that a giant surveillance aerial vehicle would provide on future battlefield situations. So the research continues and the public continues to report UFOs.

Of course, not all UFO cases can be easily explained away and that is one of the reasons the phenomenon has soaked into popular culture. The reality of UFO events is well documented. An example of this reality can be studied in the very famous Rendlesham Forest incident which occurred on the evenings of December 26 and December 27th in 1980. James Penniston was the senior security officer in charge of base security at the RAF Bentwaters/Woodbridge complex in England. James Penniston had a top-secret security clearance and he was responsible for the protection of the weapons that were stored on the base. Obviously, he was a man of impeccable trust and character. Shortly after midnight on the morning of December 26, 1980, James Penniston was told of strange lights being seen in Rendlesham Forest. It appeared that whatever the object was it apparently had recently landed. Penniston and two other officers then responded to the possible downed aircraft report. When they arrived at the site where the object had landed they observed a bright light coming from the object. The object was triangular and was estimated to be about nine feet long and 6.5 feet high. The object was sitting in a small clearing inside the woods. As the three men approached the object they began experiencing problems with their radios. An incredible amount of static electricity was in the air. No sound at all was coming from the object, and Penniston would later confirm it was unlike any craft he had ever seen before. After about ten minutes of observation, Penniston began a walk around and investigated the landed craft. He took pictures and made drawings of strange symbols he saw on the object. He touched the object which was warm and smooth. After roughly forty-five minutes the light from the craft began to intensify, and the object lifted off the ground without any noise or air disturbance. The object moved through the trees and shot off at an unbelievable rate of speed and was gone in the blink of an eye. Penniston wrote in his logbook "Speed Impossible". Because of the credibility of the witnesses of the Rendlesham Forest case it is one of the best cases in UFO history. It had physical trace evidence because three indentations remained visible in the clearing where the object had landed. A Geiger counter was used to check the site and the readings peaked in the depressions where the object had landed.

Another famous UFO event was the case of Japan Air Lines flight 1628 on November 7, 1986. A gigantic round object was seen doing impossible maneuvers. The pilot had the object on his radar and estimated the size of the object to be as big as an aircraft carrier.

Respected men like Prophecy in the News speaker Gary Stearman have experienced UFO encounters. Stearman, who comes from a family with an aviation background, was travelling in the 1960's on a solo flight to Lubbock, Texas. Gary Stearman has written that he encountered and interacted with an object that looked like an "upside down Reese's peanut butter cup". He went on to say that he actually felt waves of some sort coming from this unknown object, and he felt as if the object was probing him and reading his mind. Anyone who has ever heard Gary Stearman speak will know his sincerity and honesty, for he is truly one of the best Bible prophecy teachers on planet earth. The late Christian author Dr. Walter Martin saw a UFO and is on record testifying to the reality of the phenomena.

Obviously, there are many theories out there about the origin and nature of the UFO phenomenon. If we had to break it all down into two main camps, then we have those researchers who conclude that UFOs are visitors from another solar system, and we have researchers who say UFO's are not coming from outer space, but instead they are coming from inner space. Because of the vastness of space and the unbelievable distances between planets even in our cosmic backyard, anyone who would venture into the fringes of deep space in the future would basically have to forget about ever returning back home to friends and family. It would seem that any "flesh and blood" interstellar aliens would experience similar drawbacks in their attempts to travel to earth. To compensate for this, many researchers hypothesize that extraterrestrials travel through "wormholes" or "stargates" to visit planet earth. But if the origin for UFOs is interdimensional or extra-dimensional then the problem of our known laws of physics and distances is eliminated. Many Christians openly scoff at the thought of any serious study of UFOs, but does the Bible not speak about an extra-dimensional reality?

It is very interesting to note that two of the best known and well respected UFO researchers of the modern era are Dr. Jacques Vallee and J. Allen Hynek. Vallee was born in France and he is widely regarded as a brilliant astronomer. He was on the staff of the French Space Committee when he witnessed the destruction of tracking tapes of unknown objects orbiting the earth. This sparked his passion for the subject. Vallee arrived in the United States in 1962 and he worked with the late J. Allen Hynek. Hynek was the scientific consultant for the Air Force on their UFO investigation project called Operation Blue Book, and after years of research and several excellent books on UFOs both Hynek and Vallee reached similar conclusions on the nature and origin of UFOs.

"I believe that the UFO phenomenon represents evidence for other dimensions beyond spacetime; the UFOs may not come from ordinary space but from a multiverse which is all around us."- Jacques Vallee[5]

In 1975, after examining hundreds of cases J. Allen Hynek said this: "If UFOs are indeed somebody else's nuts and bolts hardware, then we must still explain how such tangible hardware can change shape before our eyes, vanish in a Cheshire cat manner... seemingly melt away in front of us, or apparently 'materialize' mysteriously before us without apparent detection by persons nearby or in neighboring towns. We must wonder, too, where UFOs are 'hiding' when not manifesting themselves to human eyes."[6]

It is well known in the realm of the occult that attempts to contact the "other side", or the spirit world often result in the participants experiencing strange sights of "orbs" or other light energies such as poltergeists. Can fallen angelic beings manipulate matter and create sensational displays of light and could this be the cause of some UFO phenomena? The Bible would appear to shed light on this concept.

"And no wonder! For Satan himself transforms himself into an angel of light." 2 Corinthians 11: 14[7]

Consider the following observations generally associated with a baffling UFO sighting:

1. UFOs have been seen performing right angle turns that for human pilots would be impossible.
2. UFOs seem to appear from nowhere, and then vanish without detection.
3. No sound or propulsion is observed from some UFO sightings.
4. UFOs are often seen merging into one larger object.
5. When UFOs are witnessed from a close range they can affect the immediate surroundings. The insects seem to stop making noise, time appears to slow down, and sometimes the observer experiences a feeling of entering another dimension not associated with our atmosphere, and even "missing time" can result.

6. UFOs have been known to affect electrical equipment and have cut off car engines.

This now brings us to the portion of this book that will be the strangest and darkest subject covered so far, and that is the phenomena known as "alien abductions." I have talked to several people during the course of my research who have experienced these phenomena. Let me caution the reader that I am no way an expert on this stuff and will offer no definitive answers. But there are clues and especially if you are a Christian believer, so we can find some insights into this dark subject.

When discussing the UFO phenomenon at conferences and meetings, I will usually bring up this very fundamental and logical point. If UFOs represent spaceships from visitors from other solar systems, then where are the satellite photographs of these vehicles entering the earth's atmosphere? The evidence is lacking, especially when you consider the number of UFOs reported each day. This is evidence for the interdimensional nature of the phenomena. We can carry this logic even further and go into the world of "alien abductions". I believe it is safe to say that currently aliens are not hovering over homes and beaming individuals up into spaceships in a consistent pattern. If this was really happening in real time, then it would surely be an undeniable thing to ignore, especially when you consider the vast numbers of people who claim they are being abducted. In 1997, bestselling author Whitley Strieber on the Art Bell Coast to Coast radio program stated that he had received nearly 300,000 letters by people who shared that they have had an abduction experience. So the question persists, what is happening to these individuals?

The most common reported abduction event would sound a lot like the following account: the abductee appears to awaken from a deep sleep; beings are then seen in the room and perhaps at the end of the bed, these entities communicate telepathically with reassuring words and sometimes threatening words. The abductee senses leaving the sleeping area to another location, the abductee enters a holding area and sometimes other humans are seen here. Experiments involving the sexual organs are often reported, and then the abductees are often shown in holographic fashion disturbing images of war, worldwide disasters, and sometimes they are told they have been chosen for a higher purpose. Sometimes the abductee will be told that the religions we have on planet earth are incorrect, and the truth will soon be coming out for the world to be enlightened.

There have been events reported that did happen outside, and probably the most famous case of the modern era would be the Betty and Barney Hill story from September 19, 1961. While driving in the White Mountains of New Hampshire, the couple allegedly saw an enormous disc shaped object with two rows of windows descending from the sky. They tried to evade the object but the car began to vibrate. They came to what appeared to be a roadblock, and they were taken aboard the craft against their will. They said they were given embarrassing medical experiments by a crew of hairless entities with large heads, large eyes, and grayish skin. Barney Hill reported that sperm had been taken from him, and Betty was examined and given a pregnancy test. The Hill's would later undergo regressive hypnosis and Betty and Barney's accounts were similar. A major motion picture and many books have been released about the Betty and Barney Hill event, and there have been other accounts similar to the Betty and Barney Hill abduction case.

A common explanation to the many reports of "alien abductions" is the disorder known as sleep paralysis. This condition is characterized by an individual either falling asleep or coming out of a deep sleep and experiencing the inability to move. This disorder is often associated by terrifying visions and the sense of an intruder in the room, in which the victim is unable to defend against. It is believed by many that sleep paralysis goes way back even into the middle ages when people reported incubus and demons terrorizing them while they were sleeping. So are we to conclude that the vast majority of typical "alien abductions" are simply episodes of the common disorder called sleep paralysis? Are they just vivid nightmares and bad lucid dream experiences? The answer to these above questions in my opinion is "yes", but that does not resolve the underlying prevalence of reported abduction accounts.

Sleep disorders would be a good possible answer for the typical abduction scenario, but maybe not for the cases reported in which the individuals were driving in their cars. A very strange event occurred in 1918, and for the purpose of abduction research I believe this event was critical. The famous occultist, Aleister Crowley attempted a ritual called the Amalantrah Working and according to Crowley the result of this occult ritual was a presence which manifested itself. He called the being "Lam" and he also drew a picture of the entity. The picture is a striking portrait of what our culture would later describe as an "alien grey." Chuck Missler and Mark Eastman are Christian authors who together wrote the bestseller, "Alien Encounters: The Secret Behind the UFO Phenomenon" which was released in 1997, and here is a telling quote from their book:

"Abductee surveys have revealed that the overwhelming majority of abductees have shown an interest in paranormal activities, Eastern religions, and New Age world-view. A large percentage of abductees have also reported a history of involvement with Ouija boards, astrology, witchcraft, astral projection, telepathic communication, channeling, past life regressions, and the like. Still others simply agreed to go along with their abductors when approached."[8]

I remember attending a UFO conference in Charlotte, North Carolina and a woman was interviewed about her experiences of actually seeing entities in her house. During the course of her interview she mentioned in passing that her young son and some neighbor kids used to play with an Ouija board in the house. I had to bite my lip when she said this, for it was the key ingredient to her problem. Another man then spoke about repeated abductions he was undergoing, and that the entities described themselves as "Shining ones". In Genesis chapter three, the translation for serpent is the Hebrew word (Nachash) which literally means, "Shining one". I had to bite my lip again. We are told in the New Testament to "resist the devil" and if we engage in occult activities we are in a very real sense asking for paranormal trouble to come our way. In many satanic cult groups, it is reported that often entities manifest openly and regularly instruct the members on tasks to carry out and perform. People coming out and trying to get free from Satanic Ritual Abuse often seem to have multiple personalities, and this would be similar to the accounts in the Bible when many demons would be cast out of individuals. So in some instances maybe there is more to an abduction event than simply sleep paralysis? I believe in the dark world of the occult and in Satanic Ritual Abuse cases which are often similar to what is reported in abductions, we are seeing the manifestations of fallen angelic beings. Some accounts from the Scriptures shed light on this subject and let us begin with a fascinating paranormal experience that happened to the Apostle Paul:

"I know a man in Christ who fourteen years ago-whether in the body I do not know, or whether out of the body I do not know, God knows-such a one was caught up to the third heaven. And I know such a man-whether in the body or out of the body I do not know, God knows- how he was caught up into Paradise and heard inexpressible words, which is not lawful for a man to utter." 2 Corinthians 12: 2-4[9]

The man Paul is speaking of in this Scripture most agree is himself, notice how he struggles whether this was a real, actual experience or some sort of "vision" or dream sequence. The third heaven Paul was permitted to enter briefly is called Paradise and it is where God dwells. The first heaven is our atmosphere and the second heaven is outer space. In the book of Hebrews, we are told that Jesus has passed through the heavens and is now at the right hand of the Father in Paradise.

The reported ability of today's "aliens" with that of angels in the Bible is pretty interesting. It would appear that angels from Scripture and our "alien" visitors today have the ability to manipulate matter, and they have the ability to miraculously pass right through a door or wall. Many abduction accounts include the entity seeming to pass through solid objects. In the book of Acts chapter twelve and verses five through ten, we have the account of Peter being freed from prison by an angel. Peter was under maximum security and was watched by four squads of soldiers of four men each that rotated in three hour shifts. Both of Peter's wrists were chained up and he had a guard on each side of him. Outside the cell, two more guards stood watch. The angel that helped Peter escape appeared right next to him, a light shone in the prison and Peter's chains were miraculously unchained. The angel then led Peter out of the prison undetected by any of the guards who were standing right there when this happened. Peter thought the whole event was a vision. Did the angel that freed Peter "freeze time" to do the task of releasing Peter from the prison? Remember after the crucifixion of Jesus, when the disciples were together in the upper room with all the doors locked, Jesus suddenly appeared before them in His glorified state. He did not need to knock. A woman who was going through the trauma of abduction once told me that her husband always just sleeps through the entire terrible ordeal. Could it be the world of the supernatural is not bound by the laws of physics?

Another common characteristic in abduction lore is the theme by abductees of being shown what appear to be holographic images displaying future events like war, famine, and civil unrest. Often the entities force abductees against their will to watch these disturbing images. What could be the reason for this? This brings to mind the third temptation attempt of Satan when he was with Jesus in the wilderness.

"Again, the devil took Him up on an exceedingly high mountain, and showed Him all the kingdoms of the world and their glory. And he said to Him, "All these things I will give You if You will fall down and worship me." Matthew 4: 8-9[10]

How did Satan "show" Jesus all the kingdoms of the world and all their glory? Satan could not have done this in real time; this temptation it would appear would have to be some sort of visionary experience. Indeed, the Bible is in many ways a collection of visionary episodes. Ezekiel's vision of the four living creatures in Ezekiel chapter one was certainly not a UFO. Ezekiel encountered the glorious throne of the living God as it descended before him. If someone was standing right beside the prophet, they very well could have not seen anything for the vision was meant for Ezekiel. In the book of Revelation, John saw basically the same vision as Ezekiel did when he was called up to heaven. It is incredible to think about, but the entire book of Revelation is a glorious vision. I have talked to individuals who see repeated UFOs in the sky and they often wonder why no one else around them is looking at them. This is a possible indication of the deceptive nature of the UFO phenomenon to the people it affects.

In UFO news you will most certainly not hear about on "Ancient Aliens" or any other secular paranormal program is the story that appeared in the July-September 2011 issue of Creation Magazine, which is published by Creation Ministries International.[11] The story featured former MUFON state section director from the state of Florida Joe Jordan. Investigating alleged abduction cases with his partner investigator Wes Clark the two men began their own research group called CE4, which mainly focused on close encounters of the fourth kind. Joe Jordan quickly saw the damage that experiencers were encountering and a Christian friend told the two men that they were dealing with the "spiritual realm". This friend also shared the gospel message and as a result Joe Jordan became a Christian, and his research is nothing short of remarkable. Joe Jordan's research began to show that abduction episodes could be stopped by calling on the name of Jesus Christ. People praying during an abduction event would also stop the experience. Joe Jordan began contacting fellow researchers and he found that many of them also had stories from people of abductions being stopped by praying or calling out the name of Jesus Christ. But because the conclusions were "religious" and not scientific this research was often ignored, or simply not talked about by secular researchers. The research in many cases was intentionally ignored and actually hidden. You hear often in the world of UFO research of cover ups by the government of alleged crash sites, underground bases, cattle mutilations, alien implants, and the list goes on and on. Abductions being stopped by calling on the name of Jesus Christ, now there is a cover up that is prevalent in the UFO community itself. Many secular researchers would never welcome such claims because it would rule out "flesh and blood" extraterrestrials as the culprits of abductions and space nappings. It would also stop the need to convince people to seek out regression hypnosis to find hidden answers to their abduction encounters. To put it simply, many UFO researchers would take a hit in the wallet if they promoted that abductions could be terminated by faith in Jesus Christ. Joe Jordan's research has been highlighted in many Christian publications and that is welcome news on the disturbing phenomena called "alien abductions". The article goes on to say that Joe Jordan has worked with over 400 people who have testified to having their abduction experiences stopped in the name of Christ.

One of the first things that really opened my eyes when I began my research was just how widespread the abduction phenomenon really is. Many polls suggest that thousands of people claim to be having abduction episodes. This is actually a huge mission field, but unfortunately, it has been my experience that most of the organized church has its head stuck firmly in the sand on this issue. I have had people tell me they tried to get help from a pastor or church group in hopes of trying to get solid answers to what was happening to them. These people were frustrated that they were not dealt with seriously, or that no effort to counsel them would result from talking to these church leaders. Say what you like about the abduction phenomenon, but it does ruin people's lives. Individuals will often retreat from friends or family, and become isolated and lonely. Others go from researcher to researcher seeking the next "revelation" to what they are experiencing. Lost jobs and broken families often result, and a complete lack of belief in God soon follows because they are convinced that their abductors are indeed their creators. That is what the entities have told them in many cases. Just to tell someone going through the awful trauma of abduction experiences that they are dealing with demons stops way short of what God would have us do in regards to the people affected. A great Bible verse to share would be this one:

"Beloved, do not believe every spirit, but test the spirits, whether they are of God; because many false prophets have gone out into the world. By this you know the Spirit of God: Every spirit that confesses that Jesus Christ has come in the flesh is of God, and every spirit that does not confess that Jesus Christ has come in the flesh is not of God. And this is the spirit of the Antichrist, which you have heard was coming, and is now already in the world." 1 John 4: 1-3[12]

Almost without exception the messages being delivered to abductees is that Christianity is an outdated belief system with many errors associated with it. I remember meeting an individual who had been dealing with abduction experiences her entire adult life, and it was actually a family trauma for her mother suffered as well. As I sat across from her she could not even look me in the eye, and her voice was so soft I could hardly understand her words. She looked like she had not slept through the night in quite some time. As we were talking, I just casually mentioned if she had experienced seeing anyone with "red hair" during one of her experiences. This is a common occurrence in abductions. Her eyes opened up and I think she realized I was sincere and had done my homework. I know the vast majority of our secular and Christian society scoffs at the contents of this chapter, but to suggest that Christians should not get involved with UFO research, as I have heard more than once is really a comment that lacks biblical wisdom. I think some people "get" why Christians should not turn away from the subject of UFOs.

The big debate about "alien abductions" in the Christian research community revolves around just how one interprets the exact cause of the abduction experience. Some researchers contend that the entire scope of what we would call an abduction event is visionary. Fallen angelic beings are invading the minds of thousands of individuals and the result is very lucid dream like experiences that society has come to call an alien abduction. Throw in the very common disorder called sleep paralysis, and the false memories being produced in individuals through regressive hypnosis sessions, and add it all up, and there are your causes for people thinking they are being abducted and taken aboard UFOs. And also being subject to what they believe are extremely horrifying and traumatic events, so does this answer solve the mystery of alien abductions? I do think the majority of experiences that we call "alien abductions" are simply bad lucid dreams, sleep paralysis, and visionary episodes. Does that end the discussion; no it does not.

On the other side of the coin are those researchers who see the "alien abduction" phenomenon as a fulfillment of the passage in Daniel chapter 2 and verse 43. We studied that passage in the last chapter and have asked the question of who are "they" that will mingle with the seed of men? Are they aliens? Are they celestial beings that are actually abducting individuals and taking them to the second heaven (outer space)? They are apparently engaging in terrible experiments, and even conducting hybrid breeding programs for the possible purpose of releasing these satanic hybrid creatures during the last days of earth's history right before Jesus returns. Will this be the return of the Nephilim in the last days? Jesus said the last days would be just like the days of Noah (Luke 17:26) . So you can ask yourself what was it that made the days of Noah so unique in the biblical narrative and one of the answers would be the appearance of the "sons of God" and the Nephilim from Genesis chapter 6. Does the "alien abduction" phenomenon fulfill the words of Jesus? Let us be really honest with ourselves, for we know without a doubt that intelligent evil is alive and well. We also know that demonic forces are active in all corners of our world. We often hear of the detestable practices being carried out in the many satanic cult groups that actively worship Satan and his emissaries. Are we to doubt that satanic rituals will not result in the manifestation of a fallen angelic being? These entities it has been reported can shape-shift and even walk through walls. Could they not also manifest openly and perpetrate an abduction experience to an unsuspecting victim? I admit very candidly that the thought of an actual breeding program being carried out by celestial entities on human beings is a very hard pill to swallow. For all the researchers who claim to have proof of this with their implant removals, and other various bits of evidence which surfaces from time to time we must remain logical. Incredible claims do require incredible proof and certainly so far not too many scientists are giving any validity to the implant removals, and some of the other evidence that has surfaced with abductions. Yet many Christian missionaries who are active in underdeveloped countries where the occult is being openly practiced will tell of encountering the very real effects of the demonic realm. A pastor once told me of a visit to a couple's house in which he witnessed firsthand lamps and other inanimate objects moving on their own. A presence was in the house and it was not a good one. I would caution anyone who wants to limit what could be happening and also what may happen in the future. If you take the face value approach to Scripture interpretation then the Bible testifies to the fact that celestial beings came to earth in the days before the flood, and they impregnated women and the result of this widespread act was the Nephilim. The Sethite view of all this is a result of those who want to limit what intelligent evil is capable of producing. Please hear the words of probably the most frightening passage in all of God's word:

"The coming of the lawless one is according to the working of Satan, with all power, signs, and lying wonders, and with all unrighteous deception among those who perish, because they did not receive the love of the truth, that they might be saved. And for this reason God will send them strong delusion, that they should believe the lie, that they all may be condemned who did not believe the truth but had pleasure in unrighteousness." 2 Thessalonians 2: 9-12[13]

Jesus said that deception would be a major indication that His return was near. I believe the UFO phenomenon will be a part of this deception. Some Scientists believe that one of Saturn's moons called Europa has a vast layer of liquid water beneath its surface. If the discovery is made of microbial life, it would no doubt open up discussion doubting the book of Genesis. In Mountain View, California we have the SETI Institute, and their impressive Allen Telescope Array which is a large number of small dishes pointed to the heavens above. This radio astronomy is hoping to receive communication from an alien civilization in the future. Who knows what they will contact in the days ahead? The ultimate deception would be the actual arrival of space beings on our planet, and their announcement that they were our creators. Does this sound a little impossible to you, my friend? The Bible says this deception is worldwide, and if the Bible is correct then it has happened before.

From the Living Bible........

"Now a population explosion took place upon the earth. It was at this time that beings from the spirit world looked upon the beautiful earth women and took any they desired to be their wives. Then Jehovah said, "My Spirit must not forever be disgraced in man, wholly evil as he is. I will give him 120 years to mend his ways." In those days, and even afterwards, when the evil beings from the spirit world were sexually involved with human women, their children became giants, of whom so many legends are told." Genesis 6: 1-4[14]

The same spirit world spoken of in the above translation of Genesis 6 is still with us. The earth has been visited in the past by non human beings. The earth is being visited now by non human entities, but they are not flesh and blood extraterrestrials. They are fallen angelic celestial beings whose purpose is to lead as many individuals as they can away from faith in Jesus Christ.

Conclusion

Well, I think I have covered almost everything "Nephilim related". No.... Hang on a second; there is the Nephilim/Bigfoot connection, and the conspiracy that mad scientists are splicing genes somewhere deep underground for the purpose of constructing modern Nephilim.... And then there are current popular movies and entertainment that focus on celestial beings falling in love with human females, think Twilight saga here....Maybe I will cover all this in a sequel. Shades of Genesis 6?

I agree, the Nephilim do make for good speculation, but ancient writings do speak of giants. The ancient Egyptians feared the Anakim in Canaan. Execration texts dated between 1900 and 1700 B.C. actually record curses on Anakim chieftains who dwelled in the land of Canaan. The Bible also speaks of giants.

"The other king was Og king of Bashan and his territory, who was of the remnant of the giants, who dwelt at Ashtaroth and at Edrei," Joshua 12: 4[1]

I realize that most Churches would not touch the contents of this book with a 10 foot pole, but I stand by my methods of Scripture interpretation. They are tried and true and although I am very human and grammatically challenged, I am convinced that the arguments and speculation made in this book are worthy for Christians to consider.

I openly admit it takes a whole lot of faith these days to believe in biblical creation. But to believe that life began by chance, or because of an errant asteroid that crashed to earth and spread life starting microorganisms everywhere takes a whole lot of faith as well.

This book has described a "cosmic war"....

You may say it is not a war I signed up for....

A fair objection to the Christian faith would be the argument that over the course of history thousands upon thousands have died without ever hearing the name of Jesus Christ. Are they in Hell now through no fault of their own, for they never heard the only name by which they could be saved?

Jesus commanded the gospel go to the entire world....

What if there was a Bible passage that said bluntly that if you never hear the name of Christ then when you die, you will be safe, on your way to heaven by default. Think of how damaging that verse would be, because then Christian missionaries travelling to the most remote places trying to spread the gospel would be in reality putting their subjects under condemnation. These people would have been justified if only they had never heard the gospel. My point is this, everything that is recorded in the Bible is there for a big reason, and the opposite is true as well, everything that appears to be left out of the Bible has a reason behind it also. God is ultimate justice and He will deal with apparent contradictions in the most perfect and fair way ever known to the universe.

One can never put a true measure on the way our society has benefitted from the standards and morals put forth in the Bible. Many hold religion to blame for the problems of mankind down through the ages and Jesus would agree, just read about the Pharisees and Sadducees of His day. Jesus refusal to accept the modern religion of His time was one of the reasons He was killed.

True Christianity will never be measured by the latest legislation in the Southern Baptist Convention, or the latest scandal within the halls of the Vatican. Showing up on Sunday morning and occupying a seat falls way short of what God wants from His followers.

I am reminded of a story I once heard of settlers who arrived on the Fiji Islands....

When they arrived they were apologetic to the people there for they knew that Christian missionaries had preceded them....

Sorry you had to hear the ramblings of those spreading myths and fables....

The settlers were then told that the people of the island had converted to Christianity because of the efforts of the missionaries who arrived before them. In fact, the people of the island used to be cannibals, so the settlers ought to be thankful, for if not for the missionaries they would soon be the evening meal....

I paraphrased the story, but there is a great truth in that account. My friend, it is not or ever has been about religion, or doing good deeds, or being a good person, or obeying what this priest says, or what this pastor says.

It is about a relationship with Jesus Christ....

I attended a conference not that long ago and began a conversation with a fellow researcher. She was extremely intelligent, personable, and fun to talk to....

We found out we had a lot in common, we liked the same kind of music, worked in similar fields, had similar quirks, and so the conversation went....

She knew I was a Christian so when she said she thought Jesus must have had a wife, she gave me an inquisitive look, but I said nothing....

She then went on to say that she thought Jesus never really wanted to be worshiped by men, again I said nothing....

Upon leaving the conference, I got in my car and shut the door and immediately became very ill, within seconds I had to open the car door and throw up. I think Jesus was telling me that I just blew it, really bad! But because of my relationship with Christ I was able to benefit from that event, every believer has stories of triumph and disappointment. Even someone as great as the apostle Paul spoke of times when he blew it.

"For the good that I will to do, I do not do; but the evil I will not to do, that I practice." Romans 7: 19[2]

My friend, I hope you will consider the claims of Christ.

"Jesus said to him, "I am the way, the truth, and the life. No one comes to the Father except through Me." John 14: 6[3]

Notes and Scripture References

INTRODUCTION

1. Theodor H. Gaster, The Dead Sea Scriptures (Garden City, New York: Doubleday and Co., Inc., 1956), p. 257.
2. Daniel 10: 13
3. Ephesians 6: 12

CHAPTER 1

1. Job 38: 4-7
2. Ezekiel 28: 14-15
3. Isaiah 14: 12-14
4. Luke 10: 18
5. Revelation 12: 7-9
6. Genesis 3: 15
7. Lyrics taken from Bruce Springsteen (Nebraska), released September 30, 1982 (Columbia Records), Producer: Bruce Springsteen.

CHAPTER 2

1. Steven Greer quote taken from Ancient Aliens (The Return) from Season 1, Episode 5. Original date (May 25, 2010). Copyright 2012 A and E Televisions Networks, LLC—All Rights Reserved. Distributed by Prometheus Entertainment.
2. Genesis 6: 1-4

3. Job 1: 6
4. Job 2: 1
5. Psalm 29: 1
6. Psalm 89: 6
7. Jude 6-7
8. 2 Peter 2: 4-6
9. 1 Peter 3: 19-20
10. Hebrews 13: 2
11. Flavius Josephus, The Antiquity of the Jews, (Book 1, Chapter 3:1).
12. Genesis 6: 9
13. Genesis 10: 8
14. Thomas R. Horn, Nephilim Stargates The Year 2012 and the Return of the Watchers, (Anomalos Publishing House), p. 24-25.

CHAPTER 3

1. 2 Timothy 3: 16-17
2. Daniel 4: 13
3. Translated by R.H. Charles, The Book of Enoch, (SPCK Publishing), p. 34-35.
4. Refer to the Book of Enoch, Chapter 15: 8-9. (The Book of Enoch translated by R.H. Charles, SPCK Publishing. First published in 1917, SPCK, London.)

CHAPTER 4

1. Genesis 15: 16
2. Deuteronomy 18: 10-12
3. Deuteronomy 32: 17
4. Genesis 14: 5
5. Deuteronomy 2: 10-11
6. Numbers 13: 23

7. Numbers 13: 32-33
8. Deuteronomy 2: 20
9. Numbers 14: 36-38
10. Deuteronomy 3: 11
11. Deuteronomy 3: 6
12. Joshua 11: 22
13. 1 Samuel 17: 40
14. 2 Samuel 21: 20-21

CHAPTER 5

1. Cyrus Thomas, Report on the Mound Explorations of the Bureau of Ethnology, 3-730.
2. Charles DeLoach, Giants A Reference Guide from History, the Bible, and Recorded Legend, (Lanham, Maryland: Scarecrow Press, 1995) p. 147.
3. Dr. I.D.E. Thomas, The Omega Conspiracy, (Anomalos Publishing House, Crane 65663, Copyright 2008) p. 111.
4. Joe Taylor, Story Behind the Giant Human Femur Sculpture, http://mtblanco.com/TourGiantArticle.htm
5. Gertrude Landa, Jewish Fairy Tales and Legends, (New York: Bloch, 1919).
6. Amos 2: 9
7. Isaiah 26: 14
8. Kenneth S. Wuest, Word Studies in the Greek New Testament, vol. 4, (Grand Rapids: Wm. B. Eerdmans Publishing Co., 1966.) p. 241.

CHAPTER 6

1. Isaiah 46: 9-10
2. G.H. Pember, M.A., Earth's Earliest Ages and Their Connection with Modern Spiritualism and Theosophy, (Fifth Edition, Defense Publishing, Crane, MO.)

3. Matthew 24: 36-37
4. Luke 17: 26
5. Revelation 20: 1-2
6. Isaiah 66: 22-23
7. Daniel 2: 27-45
8. Revelation 17: 12
9. Daniel 9: 24
10. Daniel 9: 25
11. Daniel 9: 26
12. Daniel 9: 27
13. 2 Thessalonians 2: 1-4
14. Matthew 24: 15
15. Daniel 12: 7
16. Revelation 12: 6
17. 1 Thessalonians 4: 16-17
18. Matthew 24: 5
19. Revelation 6: 1-2
20. Matthew 24: 6-8
21. Matthew 24: 9
22. Revelation 6: 9-11
23. Matthew 24: 29-30
24. Revelation 6: 12-13
25. Isaiah 13: 9-10
26. Joel 3: 14-15
27. Revelation 9: 11
28. Isaiah 13: 1-3
29. Revelation 16: 14
30. 1 Timothy 4: 1

CHAPTER 7

1. Neil deGrasse Tyson, Death By Black Hole and Other Cosmic Quandaries, (W.W. Norton and Company New York, 2007) p. 229.

2. Psalm 115: 16
3. Thomas Paine, The Age of Reason, (Secaucus: Citadel Press, 1974) p. 90.
4. Colossians 1: 16
5. Jacques Vallee, Dimensions: A Casebook of Alien Contact, (New York, NY: Contemporary Books, 1988) p. 284.
6. J. Allen Hynek, The Edge of Reality, (NTC/ Contemporary Publishing 1976) p. 12-13.
7. 2 Corinthians 11: 14
8. Chuck Missler and Mark Eastman, Alien Encounters: The Secret Behind the UFO Phenomenon. (Koinonia House, 1997) p. 109.
9. 2 Corinthians 12: 2-4
10. Matthew 4: 8-9
11. Creation Magazine, Vol. 33, No. 3, 2011. Lifting The Veil On The UFO Phenomenon. Article written by Gary Bates. Creation Ministries International, Publishers of Creation magazine and Journal of Creation.
12. 1 John 4: 1-3
13. 2 Thessalonians 2: 9-12
14. Genesis 6: 1-4 taken from The Living Bible, (Copyright 1971 by Tyndale House Publishers, Inc., Wheaton, Illinois 60189. All rights reserved.)

CONCLUSION

1. Joshua 12: 4
2. Romans 7: 19
3. John 14: 6

About the Author

Steve McGee lives with his wife of 23 years, Paula, in North Carolina. He welcomes the opportunity to discuss the topics covered in this manuscript with any Church or Bible Study Group. He can be contacted at: stvmcgee85@gmail.com

CPSIA information can be obtained
at www.ICGtesting.com
Printed in the USA
FFOW04n1805171014
8171FF

9 781490 838656